Bride-

TO-BE

A DEVOTIONAL JOURNAL

JANICE THOMPSON & RANDI MORROW

BARBOUR
PUBLISHING

To Megan and Kevin.
May your "big day" be the best ever!

For this cause shall a man leave his father and mother,
and shall be joined unto his wife, and they two shall be one flesh.

EPHESIANS 5:31 KJV

Published by Barbour Publishing, Inc., P.O. Box 719, Uhrichsville, Ohio 44683, www.barbourbooks.com

Our mission is to publish and distribute inspirational products offering exceptional value and biblical encouragement to the masses.

Member of the
Evangelical Christian
Publishers Association

Printed in India.

INTRODUCTION

"For I know the plans I have for you,"
declares the LORD, "plans to prosper you and not to harm you,
plans to give you hope and a future."

JEREMIAH 29:11

Welcome, bride-to-be! This exciting devotional has been created with you in mind. With the big day coming, you're sure to have plenty of questions and concerns. These daily devotionals are meant to point you in the direction of the One who has all of the answers you will ever need.

Weddings are glorious, blissful events. They can also be a little stressful. There are flowers to choose, invitations to design, cakes to sample, and dresses to try on. There are guests to invite, pastors to employ, caterers to contemplate, and a wedding party to pacify.

Whew! So much to think about. That's why it's more important than ever to stay focused on your relationship with your future mate and grounded in your relationship with the Lord.

So how do you know where to begin? After all, there are so many decisions to make, so many plans to set in motion. This book has been designed to ease your mind by walking you through the process with the Lord at the very center of your plans.

As you take time each day to read one of these devotions, take a deep breath! Ah, doesn't that feel better? Relax! Take a few moments of quiet time, away from the chaos of wedding planning. Put everything in realistic perspective. Keep the Lord in His proper place. According to the Word of God, your plans are destined to succeed as long as you do that. He wants to give you a hope and a future—together!

And remember, you're planning far more than a wedding. You are planning for a marriage—a lifetime together. This isn't just about the "big day." It's about the "big life." And that life will be all the more wonderful if Jesus Christ is kept in the very center of it.

Be blessed, bride-to-be. Be blessed!

SECTION ONE:

ONE PLUS ONE EQUALS THE TWO OF YOU

*If two lie together, then they have heat:
but how can one be warm alone?*

ECCLESIASTES 4:11 KJV

Perhaps you spent much of your adult life searching for the "perfect" person to come along. Surely you prayed, sought, and wondered—all in hopes of discovering your mate. Maybe as a little girl you dreamed of your wedding day and wondered who your Prince Charming would be. How funny, to think the Lord knew your perfect mate all along! He has been preparing the heart of your spouse-to-be from the day he was born. Your fiancé may not have ridden in on a white stallion, but he's the man for you.

And now the two of you are about to become one. Congratulations on your upcoming day! You'll have great fun getting to know each other in this exciting season of your lives together. You will have questions to answer, decisions to make, and perhaps even a few controversies to settle. That's what happens when two very different people merge into one!

And speaking of merging. . .you've always known that one plus one equals two. But now you're coming to understand the mystery of God's mathematics! According to the Word of God, one plus one equals one flesh. That means the two of you are literally one in God's sight. Amazing, when you think about it. And yet you are still two very different personalities, often with different agendas. How does that work?

Truthfully, the only way it works is with God in control. You're in a season of compromise, bride-to-be! The engagement period is one of great joy and togetherness. Over the next few weeks and months, you will discover how to think like a couple, how to merge financial matters, and how to seek the Lord together. In short, you're learning how to be "one"—and one is a lot of fun!

So as you sweep your Prince Charming into your arms, remember that with all of his flaws, all of his imperfections, he's the one God had in mind all along. And the two of you are about to set out on an amazing life together.

GOD'S IDEA OF THE IDEAL

Let every man have his own wife,
and let every woman have her own husband.

1 CORINTHIANS 7:2 KJV

When you think about the perfect mate, the word *ideal* comes to mind, doesn't it? The very definition of the word probably brings a smile to your face: "conforming to an ultimate standard of perfection or excellence" (www.dictionary.com). Ah, the ideal man. The ultimate picture of perfection! Of course, Prince Charming is the classic ideal, the one every little girl dreams of finding one day. He is our ultimate fairy-tale dream come true. And now that your Prince Charming has made his entrance, you have every reason to believe he is God's ideal man for you. No, he's not perfect. Neither are you. But the Lord desires your union to be just as fanciful, just as sweet, as any fairy tale.

Did you realize your heavenly Father knew all along what you were looking for in a mate? It's true! And His plans were even greater than your own. Sure, you probably had a list of what you'd hoped to find, but God had a list, too. The kind of ideal mate He had in mind for you was far superior to what you had in mind.

So what is God's idea of the ideal? Simple. Someone who will love you the way Christ loved the church. Someone who will provide spiritual leadership in your home and who will lead by example. Someone who cherishes you and would give his life for you.

God knew exactly what you needed when He picked your mate. He knew your good traits and bad. He knew your quirks, your personality, your habits, and your mannerisms. And He had the ideal man in mind for you.

Lord, thank You for bringing the ideal man into my life.

When did you first know your fiancé
was the right one for you?

_____

_____

_____

_____

_____

_____

_____

_____

_____

_____

_____

_____

_____

_____

Two "Wholes" = One "Holy" Union

"So they are no longer two, but one."

MARK 10:8

Some people believe they can never be whole without finding that special someone. This is a problem on many levels. For one thing, no one can fill every need. And ultimately, no one can fill the "God hole" in every human heart.

In truth, God wants us to be content in our relationship with Him before taking on the responsibility of a relationship with someone else. The strongest possible union begins with two "whole" people. When you come together as complete individuals, you will be a powerful force to be reckoned with. Sadly, many join hands and hearts while still incomplete as individuals, making for a weak marriage.

To be whole means to be wholly dependent on God—to be free from sin's sting and from the things that hold you back from serving the Lord. To be whole also means that you are listening to His voice and walking daily with Him. In other words, it means you're thriving spiritually as an individual, even without the input of the man you love. You're healthy and strong.

So can you imagine how much stronger you will be when you come together? Two people—each already powerful in faith—*combining* that faith. You'll be amazed!

The Bible teaches that a threefold cord is not quickly broken: you, your spouse, and God.

During this engagement period, take time to work on your own spiritual life, and encourage the one you love to do the same. Be as strong as you possibly can as individuals, then watch the Lord move miraculously as you come together, combining your faith!

_____

_____

_____

_____

_____

_____

_____

_____

_____

_____

_____

_____

Dear God, I want to know You more.
Today I give You all of my heart, spirit,
and soul as we spend these precious moments together.

Do you and your fiancé spend time praying together? If so, how has doing this benefited your relationship?

_____

_____

_____

_____

_____

_____

_____

_____

_____

_____

_____

_____

_____

_____

GOD'S COMPLEMENT

All beautiful you are, my darling;
there is no flaw in you.

SONG OF SOLOMON 4:7

The word *complement* is defined as "something that completes or makes perfect" (www.dictionary.com). God, with His awesome sense of humor, usually pairs us up with the very person who has all of the attributes we're missing. When someone with a strong personality, for example, marries someone a little more on the meek side, they balance each other out.

So what are your strengths, bride-to-be? What are your weaknesses? Do you manage finances well but find yourself struggling in the kitchen? Do you excel at decorating but bomb when it comes to fix-it jobs? Likely your fiancé can handle many of the chores you can't, and vice versa! And think about this from a spiritual vantage point, too. Perhaps your strength is studying the Word of God and your fiancé's is spending time in prayer. What a great team you will make!

Your husband-to-be is God's idea of the perfect complement to your personality. As you look ahead to your future together, begin to thank the Lord for sending the very person who has what you lack—and vice versa! Coming together as one will be challenging at times, no doubt, but when one of you is weak, likely the other will be strong. When one is worried, the other will be at peace.

The next several years will give you plenty of opportunities to learn from each other. Instead of grumbling over your differences, celebrate them. God, in His rich humor, planned for you to complement each other all along.

Thank You, God, for giving me my perfect complement.
I stand amazed that You knew all along just who I needed!

What personality characteristics do you and your
fiancé share? In what ways are you different?

_____

_____

_____

_____

_____

_____

_____

_____

_____

_____

_____

_____

A Strong Foundation

No one can lay any foundation other than the one already laid,
which is Jesus Christ.

1 CORINTHIANS 3:11

You've probably read the story since childhood—the one about the wise man who built his house upon the rock. The rains came tumbling down, but his house stood strong. The foolish man, on the other hand, built his house upon the sand. When the rains came, it couldn't withstand the pressure and was washed away.

The same is true with marriage. It's vitally important that you build your house upon the rock. Pray together, even now, while you're in the engagement phase. Read the Bible together. Yes, it might feel a bit odd (or even awkward) at first, but so did taking those first few baby steps. Soon enough, you will both be comfortable sharing together in this way.

Nothing is more powerful or precious than the sight of a couple praying together. And you, as a new bride, will feel strengthened by your husband's prayers. Each day's tasks will be a little easier for him if he feels your prayers, as well. What an amazing, intimate thing to share—your prayer life!

Jump the hurdle. Learn to share prayer and Bible reading times with your future spouse. Create the habit now, long before you have to deal with mortgages, babies, and family vacations. Before long, it will be a comfortable part of your daily routine, and you will feel strengthened, knowing the person God has designed for you is also agreeing with you in prayer.

_____

_____

_____

_____

_____

_____

_____

_____

_____

_____

_____

_____

Be with me, Lord, as I encourage my fiancé
to spend time with me praying and reading Your Word.
May Your presence in our lives make us stronger and draw us ever closer to You.

Will you participate in Bible study together?
If so, how will you stick to a regular
Bible reading plan?

_____

_____

_____

_____

_____

_____

_____

_____

_____

_____

_____

_____

_____

COMMUNICATION

Your lips drop sweetness as the honeycomb, my bride.

SONG OF SOLOMON 4:11

One of the biggest challenges you will face in your upcoming marriage is learning to communicate—verbally, physically, and emotionally—with your spouse in a healthy way. A facial expression can speak far more than your words ever could. So can a stance. Your emotional reactions will also communicate exactly how you feel toward him at any given moment. When you get angry or frustrated and just walk away, you are shutting down emotionally and closing yourself off—even this is a form of communication.

One of the best things you can do *before* you get married is to learn how to speak and respond to each other in a loving, healthy way. Consider going through premarital counseling so that you have a chance to develop communication skills before taking your vows. Ask your pastor or officiant to meet with you and your fiancé together for a couple of weeks prior to the wedding. During these sessions, he or she can help you discuss your differences and pinpoint any issues that may come up in your future. Your pastor can also offer valuable information and advice on how to sustain a happy and lasting marriage. Moreover, you and your fiancé will gain a friendship with your pastor or counselor that you can count on throughout your marriage and will have a safe and confidential environment to go to if you ever need help working through issues together in the future.

There are many ways to build a strong relationship before you get married, and learning to communicate with your significant other is key!

God, You are the ultimate communicator.
You show us Your love in so many ways.
Help us build good communication skills.
Show us how to strengthen this part of our relationship
so that it is the strongest it can be.

What is your idea of an ideal marriage?

_____

_____

_____

_____

_____

_____

_____

_____

_____

_____

_____

_____

_____

_____

THE FRIENDSHIP FACTOR

As iron sharpens iron, so one man sharpens another.

PROVERBS 27:17

You've probably been to a wedding for which the invitation or program read "Today I am marrying my best friend." It's a sweet sentiment, but what does it mean? Were the bride and groom childhood friends who played together and one day fell in love? Were they high school sweethearts who were first the best of friends? Perhaps this is the case for some couples, but most couples have a far different story.

Whether you have known your sweetheart for years or only a short period of time, you can develop a strong relationship with him that will ensure you are marrying your best friend. But how do you go about doing this? First of all, you have to realize that a friendship must be built and worked on continuously. It is not something that just happens in a day. When you are friends with your fiancé, you are there with him through good and bad. You know him for the person he really is, and he knows you the same way. There are no shows to put on; there is no pretending that you're someone you're not.

This God-ordained relationship will outlast the rush of infatuation. Learn to build on this friendship, as well as on your love for each other. Spend as much time talking as you can. Go out and do something fun together. Learn each other's quirks. Tell each other your hopes and dreams. Most important, pray for each other. Doing these things will build a strong friendship that will be the godly basis for your upcoming marriage.

_____

_____

_____

_____

_____

_____

_____

_____

_____

_____

_____

_____

Thank You, Lord, for providing not only a husband-to-be,
but a wonderful best friend!
Show me ways to strengthen our God-given friendship.
We will ever praise You!

How do you enjoy spending time together as a couple?

_____

_____

_____

_____

_____

_____

_____

_____

_____

_____

_____

_____

_____

WE'RE ENGAGED!

He brought me to the banqueting house, and his banner over me was love.

SONG OF SOLOMON 2:4 KJV

Have you ever studied the word *betrothal*? In biblical times, couples were betrothed, often from childhood. Their parents decided whom—and when—they would marry. The betrothal period, which lasted one year, must have been quite fascinating—especially if you were scheduled to marry someone you hardly knew or someone considerably older than yourself. During this season, the groom went to "prepare a place" for his bride, returning to fetch her when the time was right.

Your engagement to your fiancé is a bit like a betrothal, though (thankfully) the two of you were able to do the choosing. But the concept is much the same. An engagement is the period of time before the marriage, during which you settle the issue in your mind *(I'm really going to marry this man!)* and begin to make plans. This is a God-ordained season of your life, bride-to-be! It's a time for you and your fiancé to catch your breath, look to God and each other, and then look ahead to your plans for the future.

Perhaps you're eager to be married. You wish it could happen right now. You'll learn to appreciate the engagement period because it gives you time to prepare adequately for what's coming. And weddings are a lot of work—even simple ones! But the work that goes into planning a wedding is nothing in comparison to the work that goes into planning a life together. That's really what this season is about: You're getting ready for "till death do us part." And you're doing it hand in hand, with the person God selected for you before you were even born. If you can trust Him to bring the two of you together, you can certainly trust Him to help you through this crazy, romantic, work-filled, blissful season of your life.

Enjoy your engagement, bride-to-be! It is a gift. Receive it as one.

THE PROPOSAL

You have stolen my heart, my sister, my bride; you have stolen my heart with one glance of your eyes, with one jewel of your necklace.

SONG OF SOLOMON 4:9

What makes the perfect proposal? Is it the surprise factor? The location where it takes place? What is said—and how? The size of the engagement ring?

These are all factors in a great proposal, but even if the ring isn't quite what you expected, or the question is asked in a less-than-flamboyant way— even if there are no grand fireworks involved, no display on the screen at a baseball game—isn't it still the perfect proposal, simply in light of the fact that the man you love has asked you to be his. . .forever? Of course it is! Every proposal is special.

There's something precious about a man asking you to spend the rest of your life with him. He is saying that he loves you. He needs you. You make his life happier just by being in it, and he desires your love and no one else's for the rest of his life.

Isn't the love of God the same? We are His bride, and His desire is toward us. He longs for an intimate relationship with each of us. He wants us to be free to share our innermost secrets with Him. He wants to shower us with His blessings. He loves us deeply and yearns for us to love Him with that same undying love. It truly is a beautiful thing!

As you celebrate the excitement of your fiancé's proposal, remember that God has also extended you the proposal of a lifetime: a chance to be in a relationship with Him—a relationship that will last forever!

_____

_____

_____

_____

_____

_____

_____

_____

_____

_____

_____

Oh, sweet Lord, I love You so much. You fill my heart with joy.
As I snuggle up close to You today, I bring my inmost desires and thoughts
and whisper them in Your ear. Hold me close in Your arms,
my Friend, my Master, my loving God.

How did your fiancé pop the question?

_____

_____

_____

_____

_____

_____

_____

_____

_____

_____

_____

_____

_____

_____

FIRST THINGS FIRST

My lover is mine and I am his.

SONG OF SOLOMON 2:16

The moment that ring is slipped on your finger, it's real. You're engaged! What you've dreamed about and hoped for all of your life is actually happening—*right now*. You are no longer boyfriend and girlfriend. You are fiancé and fiancée! It's time to tell the world! Make your announcement, show off your ring, set a date. There's so much to do and so little time to do it. . .right?

First things first, bride-to-be. Relax; breathe! Enjoy the moment. Cherish the reality that this is your dream come true. Savor the joy of being engaged. Take some time to realize just what that means. Things are changing—and those changes are for the better.

When you were dating, you felt connected to each other. But now that you're engaged, a certain (natural) possessiveness kicks in. Why? Because the level of your commitment has deepened. Things are different now. Your relationship has solidified.

As you speed toward the wedding day, you'll learn many lessons about what it means to become one instead of two—not just in the eyes of God, but in the eyes of the world, as well. Your life isn't just about you anymore. It's about both of you together. Not just your needs, but his needs, too.

Perhaps you've lived for yourself most of your life. It's time to start thinking about two now. The word *I* will no longer drive you. From now on, it's all about "we." And "we" is a perfect place to be!

_____

_____

_____

_____

_____

_____

_____

_____

_____

_____

_____

_____

_____

Dear God, words cannot express the gratitude I feel for Your making me a fiancée!

It is one more precious gift from You that I can never repay!

Thank You, Lord, for making my dreams come true!

What was your first reaction when your fiancé proposed?

_____

_____

_____

_____

_____

_____

_____

_____

_____

_____

_____

_____

_____

SHARING THE NEWS

And there was great joy in that city.

ACTS 8:8 KJV

Once you have that engagement ring on your finger, a proposal under your belt, and the word *fiancé* on your lips, everything changes. You are filled with an amazing sense of security and satisfaction. The joy you feel is unlike anything you've experienced before. And best of all, it's God-given!

When that special someone is soon to be all ours, a natural, God-given possessiveness comes over us. We feel the need to let anyone and everyone know our thrilling news. Whether in person or by e-mail or phone, you'll want to share the excitement.

Brides and grooms, you need to be ready for the responses of those you care about. Your friends and loved ones are sure to jump on the "joy bandwagon," creating a near-frenzy at times. Mothers are prone to tears. Fathers are prone to concern about finances. Brothers and sisters are prone to ridiculous joy, total apathy, or inward jealousy (depending on their own situations). And best friends are likely to say either, "I wish I was getting married" (girls), or "There goes your freedom" (guys).

At any rate, the period immediately following the proposal is sure to be fraught with emotion, and emotions are God-given. Just don't let the frenzy overwhelm you. Take it all in stride and understand that it will surely pass. Only joy will remain.

_____

_____

_____

_____

_____

_____

_____

_____

_____

_____

_____

_____

Lord, as joy bubbles up within me, I am filled with thanksgiving.
In Your perfect timing, You have made my dreams come true!
And You planned it all while I was still in my mother's womb.
Thank You for the gift of my fiancé, my wedding, and my upcoming marriage.

With whom did you share the good news first?

Oh, That Advice!

*Discretion will protect you,
and understanding will guard you.*

PROVERBS 2:11

Now that you're engaged, you probably have countless questions running through your mind. What type of wedding do you want? Are there any good caterers in your area? How can you ensure that your relationship with your fiancé stays strong throughout the engagement?

With all of these unanswered questions, you may be feeling slightly overwhelmed, especially when well-meaning friends and family members suddenly swarm you, advising you on every conceivable thing. All of these suggestions will come at you fast and furiously.

So what's a bride-to-be to do? How can you deal with the initial shock of being inundated by friends and relatives? Simple! Smile and nod. Consider the fact that the Lord has already placed discretion and understanding within

you. Then when you're ready, decide whom you want to go to for advice. Perhaps your sisters or your mother can help you decide on your wedding specifics. Your pastor can probably help answer your relationship questions through premarital counseling. And don't forget to go to your future mother-in-law with any questions regarding your engagement or upcoming marriage. You might be surprised at the valuable information she can offer you!

Of all the people in your life who can offer their experience and advice, no one is more qualified than God. After all, He knows you and your fiancé better than you know yourselves, and He can settle any fears or concerns you may have. Just go to Him with your questions, and He will be there to walk you through each new and exciting experience!

God, You are the ultimate counselor. You know all the questions I have.
You know all the things I need to accomplish. Lead me in Your wisdom.
Fill me with Your strength. Infuse me with Your peace.

How have you handled any strong opinions about the wedding from well-meaning friends or relatives?

_____

_____

_____

_____

_____

_____

_____

_____

_____

_____

_____

_____

_____

Preparing to Leave and Cleave

Therefore shall a man leave his father and his mother,
and shall cleave unto his wife: and they shall be one flesh.

GENESIS 2:24 KJV

Brides-to-be are as varied as seashells, and so are the homes they come from. Some are tied to their families and struggle with the idea of leaving the comforts and conveniences of home. Others seem to do well with the transition.

So where do you fit in this "leaving and cleaving" spectrum? Have you already lived away from home—at college or perhaps with a roommate? Do you still live in the house you grew up in? It will certainly be harder for you to make this shift if you've never ventured far from your parental covering, but it's time to start thinking about doing so now, during the engagement period. Leaving the nest is an inevitable part of life—one you can't avoid.

What can you do in the interim? How can you make a smooth transition?

If you're still living with your mother and father, enjoy your remaining weeks and months together. Treasure the moments! Listen to their advice, but remember that your husband-to-be is now a vital part of the equation.

"Cleaving" is a little easier, because it comes naturally. Linking arms with your fiancé will be a joy, something you won't have to work very hard at. Just remember to keep the lines of communication open at all times. And if you do run into any problems (say, your parents disagree with something you and your fiancé have settled on), remember to turn to the Lord for the best advice of all. Cleave to Him first and foremost, and answers won't be long in coming!

Lord, give me comfort and strength as I venture out of my parents' nest.

Help me as I prepare to "cleave" to the man I love.

How will you adjust to living with your spouse 24/7?

_____

_____

_____

_____

_____

_____

_____

_____

_____

_____

_____

_____

_____

REALISTIC EXPECTATIONS

May he give you the desire of your heart
and make all your plans succeed.

PSALM 20:4

What are you expecting from your engagement period? It's an honest question, and one you must ask yourself. Some brides-to-be enter this season feeling invincible—sure they can handle the workload, the emotions, and the changes. Their personal expectations are high, possibly too high. Sadly, many of these frazzled females crater after only a few short weeks of trying to "do it all" and "be it all." Then they battle feelings of letdown—all because they started out with unrealistic expectations.

What about you? What are you expecting of yourself during this season? The Bible teaches us that people perish without a vision. You must set goals for yourself, especially during the engagement period. Otherwise, you might find yourself racing toward your wedding day with many things left undone. On the other hand, you need to be careful not to put too much on your plate. If you do, you're likely to find yourself exhausted and frustrated.

So plan wisely. Take advantage of the first few weeks to put everything—absolutely everything—down on paper. Lock in the things you can (the date, the location, etc.), and make a plan for how you will accomplish the rest.

According to www.dictionary.com, the word *realistic* means "based on what is real or practical." So get real, bride-to-be! And keep everything (even your hopes and dreams) on a practical level. That way you won't find yourself facing weariness or disappointment.

Lord, You know the desires of my heart.
I come to You today, asking for Your plan for my big day.
Show me Your will, and then bless my steps as I follow through—
practically and realistically.

In what ways can you keep your expectations
realistic as you go about planning
for your wedding?

_____

_____

_____

_____

_____

_____

_____

_____

_____

_____

_____

_____

_____

_____

MAKING TIME FOR EACH OTHER

He has made everything beautiful in its time.

ECCLESIASTES 3:11

You're engaged—and in full wedding-planning mode. There's so much to do and so little time to do it. You have dresses to try on, facilities to look at, and a date to choose. Perhaps your schedule is so full that you're starting to feel overwhelmed. Set aside plenty of time to spend with your fiancé. Don't let yourself forget what this wedding is really all about. It's okay—a good thing, even—to relax sometimes and just be together! Focus on the important things, especially each other.

It's worth making the time to stay centered on your relationship. It won't grow or thrive, otherwise. Sure, there are plenty of things to plan. An engagement wouldn't be an engagement without preparations, would it? But in the midst of the planning, set aside one night per week for a date night. Don't

make it a "wedding meeting." Don't be so focused on the wedding that chaos reigns. You are important to each other—more important than the plans. Remember what your engagement is all about—the two of you!

God has made everything beautiful in its time. That means He has given you this time, your engagement period, as a thing of beauty. Relish the loveliness of a quiet evening alone, and remember that God has given both of you this season—and each other—as a special gift.

Thank You, God, for the gift of my fiancé and the gift of time to spend together!
Help us to remember that in the midst of this sometimes chaotic planning,
it's not just about the wedding—it's about the love You have given us to share!

Will you continue scheduling "date nights"
even after you're married?
Why or why not?

_____

_____

_____

_____

_____

_____

_____

_____

_____

_____

_____

_____

_____

_____

SETTING PLANS IN MOTION

Commit to the LORD whatever you do,
and your plans will succeed.

PROVERBS 16:3

Once the engagement ring is securely in place and all of the important people have been told, it's only natural to want to dive right into the preparations. After all, there's so much to be done! So where do you begin?

Of course, most people start by setting a date. This isn't always the case, but it sure helps with other things—such as how long to wait before ordering invitations, what type of flowers you will choose, and so forth. And, naturally, the style and color of bridesmaids' dresses will depend, at least in part, on the season of the wedding.

You will also need to decide who will plan your wedding. Will you be doing it yourself or hiring a wedding planner? Will you call on a mother, sister, or friend to help coordinate? And where will the wedding take place? At your church? At a wedding facility? Will you provide a meal or just cake and punch?

Oh, the workload! You're bound to get caught up in the details and may even feel overwhelmed. By far the best thing you can do for yourself during this season is to take a deep breath and relax. Don't get so preoccupied with the details that you forget to enjoy your relationship. What you're planning for is not just a wedding but a life together. As many hours as you spend preparing for the wedding, spend at least that much time together, talking about your future. That way, once the big day is over, you'll be prepared for the rest of your life.

THE WEDDING PLANNER

*She sets about her work vigorously;
her arms are strong for her tasks.*

PROVERBS 31:17

The Bible doesn't mention the wedding of the Proverbs 31 woman, but one can't help but think she probably had it all together. Why hire a wedding planner when you're the Martha Stewart of your day? Who needs a seamstress when you can whip together your own dress and hand-sew thousands of imported beads? What would be the point of purchasing invitations when you happen to be an expert in calligraphy?

Perhaps, like many women, you've always been a little intimidated by the Proverbs 31 woman, but surely even *she* became a little stressed out when it came to her wedding day. Have you ever met a bride who didn't? Truthfully, there's so much to think about that even the most organized, most gifted woman on the planet can scarcely handle it all on her own. That's why so many women turn to professional wedding planners—experts

in the field. Wedding planners can take the load from your shoulders, allowing you to breathe a little easier.

If you're unable (or unwilling) to hire a professional wedding planner, then dip into your established pool of "experts." Aunt Sally bakes great cakes? Give her a call. Uncle Johnny is a whiz in the toolshed? Ask him to build that archway. You sister-in-law is an amazing decorator? Ask her to help you decorate the reception hall or make centerpieces.

Sure, all women aspire to be like the Proverbs 31 gal. But likely even she dropped into bed at night completely exhausted. In other words, pace yourself. Be willing to accept help—professional or otherwise!

_____

_____

_____

_____

_____

_____

_____

_____

_____

_____

_____

_____

_____

As I begin to accept outside help in planning for my wedding,
I thank You, Lord, for providing just the right people to work alongside me!

What has been the most stressful time during your wedding planning?

_____

_____

_____

_____

_____

_____

_____

_____

_____

_____

_____

_____

_____

GOIN' TO THE CHAPEL

Lift up your hands in the sanctuary,
and bless the LORD.

PSALM 134:2 KJV

When you think about your dream wedding, where does it take place? On a beach? In the church you grew up in? In an elaborate wedding facility? In a significant outdoor area, such as a park by a lake or a gazebo in a friend's backyard?

If you're like most brides-to-be, you'll pay particular attention to where your wedding takes place. This location will be special for many reasons. All of your lasting memories will begin here. Your photos will be taken here. And this is the place—forever etched in your mind—where your "till death do us part" vows will be spoken.

Why do you suppose weddings traditionally take place in churches or chapels? Most couples see it as a way to announce to their friends and families that they want God in the center of their ceremony. The ceremony is a holy thing, meant to be an announcement to a watching world. Many opt for a beautiful sanctuary or small chapel to set the tone. However, a seaside service or a beautiful spot in the country can be just as lovely, just as sacred.

Wherever you decide to say your "I do's," don't forget that it's more about what you're doing than where you're doing it. Sure, the location will add to the overall feel or ambience of the day, but regardless of the place, God will meet you there. And when the day has ended, you will always remember it as the place where your life changed forever.

As I begin my search for and then settle on the "perfect" place,
I thank and praise You, the perfect God, for meeting me there.

Where will your wedding ceremony take place?
Why did you select this location?

_____

_____

_____

_____

_____

_____

_____

_____

_____

_____

_____

_____

_____

FOOTING THE BILL

"Then he sent some more servants and said,
'Tell those who have been invited that I have prepared my dinner:
My oxen and fattened cattle have been butchered,
and everything is ready. Come to the wedding banquet.'"

MATTHEW 22:4

It's interesting to note that the first miracle Jesus performed was at a wedding. When He turned water into wine that day in Cana, it was the very finest. Only the best for those wedding guests! Weddings have always been lavish affairs. Why? Because they are a time for celebration—and celebrations, even in biblical days, were reasons to feast. The words "no expense spared" could probably be applied to all biblical feasts (wedding or otherwise). In other words, parents have forked over the big bucks throughout history.

So who's paying for your wedding? Your parents? His? You and your fiancé? Regardless, you'll have a lot to discuss when it comes to planning for the big day. If you're not careful, costs can get out of hand quickly, leading to disputes both within the family and between the two of you.

Start by setting a budget. Make it reasonable. Talk with your wedding planner (professional or otherwise) to double-check necessities. Make plenty of calls before you commit to caterers, florists, and so on. Above all, don't get caught in the trap of thinking you have to outdo the Joneses. If you're careful, you'll find that it's possible to pull off a lavish affair on a small budget. And remember, your guests will have a wonderful time simply because it's your big day.

The Lord loves a great celebration and wants you to have a beautiful wedding, bride-to-be. He approves of making it a very special day—for you and your guests. As always, if you keep Him at the center of your plans, it will be a remarkable day!

_____

_____

_____

_____

_____

_____

_____

_____

_____

_____

_____

_____

Give us wisdom, Lord, as we figure out a budget for our wedding.
We praise You here and now for the joyous celebration our wedding day will be!

Have you set a wedding budget?
If so, how are you doing sticking to it?

_____

_____

_____

_____

_____

_____

_____

_____

_____

_____

_____

_____

_____

_____

THE PERFECT DRESS

"Does a maiden forget her jewelry,
a bride her wedding ornaments?"

JEREMIAH 2:32

As most little girls do, you probably spent a good part of your childhood playing wedding dress-up. Maybe you slipped on your pretty white Sunday dress, perhaps using a white lace tablecloth for your veil, and proceeded to prance around the room playing the bride. You may have even had a bouquet of flowers and a make-believe groom. Nearly every girl dreams of having a fairy-tale wedding, and one of the biggest parts of that dream is having the perfect wedding dress.

There's just something about that special dress. When you find the perfect one, you immediately know that it's the dress you are meant to wear. It makes you smile. You feel like a princess when you put it on. You want to slip into it all the time, just to remember what it feels like. And on your wedding day, all eyes will be on you, in awe of the beauty and purity that you portray as a "bride adorned."

Did you ever wonder why the wedding dress carries such significance? It has spiritual relevance! The body of Christ—the church—stands as a bride adorned for her groom. We are to prepare ourselves for His return, dressing ourselves in the armor of God. We are to be Christ's pure bride, setting ourselves apart for His will.

As you prepare to find that perfect dress for your wedding day, trying on different styles until you find just the right one, remember that you are also Christ's bride. Adorn yourself in purity and cover yourself daily in God's Word, preparing yourself for your Groom's return.

Dear God, when I accepted You into my heart, I became Yours before all others.
Adorn me with Your Word and cover me with Your love each and every day
as I set myself apart for You, my Lord and Savior.

How did you feel when you first tried on "the dress"?

You Are Invited. . .

*So those servants went out into the highways,
and gathered together all as many as they found,
both bad and good: and the wedding was furnished with guests.*

MATTHEW 22:10 KJV

Putting together a wedding invitation list is a bit like playing Santa Claus. You make your list. Check it twice. Never mind who's been naughty or nice—you have no choice but to invite most of the relatives, within reason, of course.

Deciding who to invite can be a tough process. Will you invite only people who are active participants in your life? Will you include distant aunts and uncles you haven't seen in years? What if one of you has an ex with whom you are still friends? Do you invite that person to the wedding?

If you're paying for a wedding facility that charges "by the head" and you need to taper the guest list, where do you start? Your dad's boss? Your long-lost cousin? It's tough to decide!

And if you thought *making* the list was difficult, wait until you get ready to address and mail the invitations! It's quite a process, tracking down addresses, ensuring that names are spelled correctly, and double-checking that no one is inadvertently left off the list. What a lot of work! Yet how wonderful to know that so many people care about you and will want to spend your special day with you.

God is familiar with the invitation process. After all, He is our Bridegroom and has sent out invitations to all of humankind for the ultimate wedding. And the wording of the invitation can be found throughout the Bible: "You are cordially invited to a relationship with the King of kings."

It doesn't get any better than that, does it?

Thank You, Lord, for inviting me into a relationship with You,
for accepting me as Your daughter!

Have you made out the guest list?
How many guests do you plan to invite?

_____

_____

_____

_____

_____

_____

_____

_____

_____

_____

_____

_____

_____

THE WEDDING PARTY

" 'Friend,' he asked, 'how did you get in here
without wedding clothes?' "

MATTHEW 22:12

One of the most precious gifts in life is having friends and family to help you celebrate the wonderful moments. There is nothing quite like being surrounded and supported by your loved ones during an exciting and life-changing time, and your wedding day is definitely one of those times!

Whom will you choose to be in your wedding party? These are the people who will stand with you and for you, to support your decision. They're also the ones who will be there to help make your day as peaceful and fun as possible. So who are these special people? And how do you choose?

Many people will come to mind when you are choosing your bridesmaids. If you have sisters, you will probably think of them. What about your fiancé's sisters? Perhaps there is a relative who has been there for you. And, of course, you will want to consider your closest friends, especially that best friend who means so much to you. You will want the women in your wedding party to be ones you can count on if any troublesome issues arise.

You will also need to discuss your wedding party with your fiancé to work out the small details. How many people do you want or need? Who will walk with whom? Has anyone been left out? Your fiancé can help you make the final decisions before you begin asking people to be a part of your big day. Just remember to choose bridesmaids you know you can count on to be there for you. And ask God for His opinion in the matter. He will help you choose the right women to stand with you on your special day!

_____

_____

_____

_____

_____

_____

_____

_____

_____

_____

_____

_____

God, You have placed friends and family in my life
to support me during this exciting time.
Help me choose the right people to stand with me on my special day.
Thank You for blessing me with so many friendships!

Whom have you chosen to stand with you on your wedding day? Why?

_____

_____

_____

_____

_____

_____

_____

_____

_____

_____

_____

_____

_____

_____

_____

BLOWING BUBBLES

Do not be anxious about anything, but in everything,
by prayer and petition, with thanksgiving,
present your requests to God.

PHILIPPIANS 4:6

As you plan for your big day, there will be plenty of opportunities to blow bubbles (make big deals out of little ones). Perhaps your bridesmaids won't be as helpful as you'd hoped. Perhaps the invitations will come back with a misspelling, or your caterer will overcharge you for something. Maybe your fiancé will disagree with some of your choices. What will you do in situations such as these?

You'll have to work double time to keep your temper in check when these occasions arise, particularly if things are going wrong. And things *will* go wrong. Whenever you're working with a team of people, you're likely to have conflicts, even over the simplest things.

Remember, you don't have to shoulder all of the wedding-planning responsibility alone. Both you and your fiancé should be equally involved. Ask for his opinion when finalizing details. Consider giving him a special project, such as choosing the band or deejay, to give him a sense of involvement. This is his day, too, and his ideas and desires are important. Agree with some of his choices even if it means setting aside some of your own ideas about the ideal wedding.

As with the rest of life, you will have to pick your battles. There has never been a more appropriate time than now, as you face many challenges at once. If you follow the advice in the scripture above, you'll learn that it's possible to give your anxieties to God; it starts with presenting your requests to Him. Just run to Him.

_____

_____

_____

_____

_____

_____

_____

_____

_____

_____

_____

_____

Lord, I feel so stressed out today.
I come to You with a heavy load and thank You for Your willingness to carry it.
Give me wisdom with all of my decisions.
I praise You for giving me peace even in the midst of storms.

Is your fiancé involved in any part
of the wedding planning?

_____

_____

_____

_____

_____

_____

_____

_____

_____

_____

_____

_____

_____

MERGING AND CONVERGING

*God has combined the members of the body
and has given greater honor to the parts that lacked it.*

1 CORINTHIANS 12:24

According to www.dictionary.com, the word *merge* means "to combine or unite into a single enterprise, organization, body." The word *converge* means "to tend to a common result, conclusion."

Can you see how those two things are similar? Can you see how they're different?

When you merge worlds with your fiancé, you're combining everything you have into one. That means you're putting together your finances, your housing, your ideas, and your ideals! These things will all be melded together into a pot called "ours." The word *mine* will soon disappear from your vocabulary.

When you converge with your spouse, you're working toward the same goal or conclusion. In other words, you're a team—inseparable, headed in the same direction. Even if the finances don't seem to be coming together in the way you'd hoped, you still work in tandem toward a similar goal. You're never in opposition. You're always together—in everything.

So how does it feel to be a team player after spending years on your own? If you're one of those able-bodied souls who has been remarkably independent, this time in your life may be a challenge for you. Sharing the reins of power may be tough. On the other hand, if you've struggled with being on your own, marrying someone who can help make decisions and shoulder responsibilities may be a huge relief. You might have to watch out, though. Remember, the Lord wants you to come into this marriage as a healthy individual. Your union will be that much stronger if you do.

Will you find it difficult to share responsibilities and challenges with someone else? Will it be strange to share a bathroom, a checkbook, and a remote control? This whole idea of merging and converging is God's. He's all about two becoming one, as we've mentioned before. And He will give you the capability to pull it off. Get ready, bride-to-be. This part is going to be great fun!

FAMILIES

Jesus knew their thoughts and said to them:
"Any kingdom divided against itself will be ruined,
and a house divided against itself will fall."

LUKE 11:17

Back in biblical times, whole families lived together even after marriage. Can you imagine living in the same house with your siblings, in-laws, and spouse? Must've been pretty tough. Likely you're not interested in that option, but even twenty-first-century couples have to learn what it means to merge families.

Is it really possible to meld two completely different units into one, or is that the idea at all? When you take on a spouse, are you also taking on his parents, siblings, aunts, uncles, and grandparents? If you are, does that mean you have to become like them—picking up their habits and customs? More interesting still, will your parents get along with his parents? Your siblings with his siblings? Families are vastly different, after all. They have different views, opinions, and lifestyles. They often have differing faiths (even among Christians, there are a variety of denominations to quibble over). Holidays are celebrated differently. Political views can get in the way. In short, merging families can be a challenge.

As your family comes together with your fiancé's, look for common bonds. Never pit one side against the other. Don't assume that because they do things differently, they're wrong. If his mama was a good cook and you're not, ask her for help. If your traditions vary slightly, consider a compromise. Above all, remember that the Lord has included all of you in His family. He celebrates your differences, and in time, you will learn to do the same.

Thank You, God, for my new family members.
I pray that both sides of the family will soon see each other as one.

How do your families get along?
What are some of their common bonds?

_____

_____

_____

_____

_____

_____

_____

_____

_____

_____

_____

_____

_____

_____

FINANCES

*Honor the LORD with your wealth, with the firstfruits of
all your crops; then your barns will be filled to overflowing,
and your vats will brim over with new wine.*

PROVERBS 3:9–10

When you get married, God desires for you and your husband to be one—not only physically, but spiritually and emotionally, as well. He even desires for you to be one in everyday matters, such as your finances. This is probably one of the most difficult areas for an engaged couple to merge, and there is no time like the present to practice becoming one in your finances.

The best way to become one is to begin to think like one. Your finances are no longer "mine" but "ours." Make time to sit down with your husband-to-be and write out all of your bills, making note of any additional expenses you will have once you are married. Figure out your total income as a couple and write out a budget before you get married, setting boundaries for what you will spend on eating out, what you will set aside for savings, and so forth. You will also need to decide what you will keep once you are married. Will you need two vehicles, computers, or televisions? What about credit cards and other debt? You will want to know exactly what you are entering the marriage with as far as any debt is concerned.

Most important, you will need to make a tithing plan. Sit down with your fiancé to discuss how much of your income you will set aside for tithe and offerings. Placing this item at the top of your list when you make your budget will help ensure that you stay financially faithful throughout your marriage. This is the best thing you can do to get your marital finances off to a solid start. When you give God the first portion of your income, He will always take care of the rest!

_____

_____

_____

_____

_____

_____

_____

_____

_____

_____

_____

_____

_____

_____

Dear God, give us Your guidance and wisdom as we set up a budget as a couple.
We pledge to honor You by setting aside the first portion of our income as our tithe,
knowing that now and forever, You will provide us with all we need.

Have you discussed whether you or your soon-to-be
husband will handle your finances?
If so, how did you reach a decision?

_____

_____

_____

_____

_____

_____

_____

_____

_____

_____

_____

_____

_____

_____

Housing

"Long life to you! Good health to you and your household!
And good health to all that is yours!"

1 Samuel 25:6

One of the most exciting things you will do during your engagement involves locating a place to live once you are married. Many factors come into play while deciding what type of home is best for you and your husband-to-be. Perhaps you both still live at home with family, or maybe you each have your own place. Maybe you have recently graduated college with no place to call home after years of dormitory life. Perhaps you even live in separate states, and one of you will be moving after the wedding takes place. Whether you are planning to live in a house, an apartment, a town house, or some other place, you should begin to plan together for the future.

The first thing you will need to decide is what type of home you and your husband-to-be can afford. Will you be paying a mortgage or rent?

Once you make this decision, together you can begin looking for a place to call home. Make a day of it. Go out to lunch and then visit some apartments or model homes in the area where you will be living. You will want the home you choose to be a place you can call your own, where you both feel comfortable, with décor that you both like. Begin to talk with your fiancé about the things that are important to each of you when setting up your new home together.

Most important, you will want to ensure that your home is a place where God is first. Consider praying over your house or apartment together once you have chosen it. Dedicate this special place to God, and ask Him to be a part of everything that goes on there.

_____

_____

_____

_____

_____

_____

_____

_____

_____

_____

_____

_____

_____

_____

_____

Dear Lord, when my fiancé and I find that special place to call home,
may You and Your love be ever present there.
And may our years in our new home begin with us saying,
"As for me and my house, we will serve the LORD" (Joshua 24:15 KJV).

Have you and your fiancé chosen where
you will live after you're married?
If so, what factors affected your decision?

_____

_____

_____

_____

_____

_____

_____

_____

_____

_____

_____

_____

_____

_____

Thoughts and Beliefs

*If on some point you think differently,
that too God will make clear to you.*

Philippians 3:15

The engagement period is a great time to get to know—*really* get to know—the thoughts and beliefs of your spouse-to-be. Even if you've both been raised in church and have solid relationships with the Lord as individuals, there are bound to be a few doctrinal differences, particularly if you were raised in different denominations. Perhaps you prefer a more contemporary service, while he's all about traditional. Maybe you like an old-fashioned steeple and stained-glass windows, but he prefers a contemporary coffee shop/marketplace ministry.

Early on, you will have to determine which issues are eternal and which are noneternal. Some things really are critical and are not up for debate: believing in Jesus as Savior and agreeing to raise your children in a Christian home, for example. Others are not: nine o'clock service versus eleven o'clock, for example. It's easy to see that you have to pick your battles. And look on the bright side—if you try new things, you might find that you prefer them to the old.

Differences in thoughts and beliefs aren't limited to church-related issues, either. You and your spouse-to-be are bound to have other differences of opinion, too—such as where you should live, what kind of car you should drive, and whether your (potential) children should go to public school or private. Yep, it's time to merge and converge those noneternals. Learn to compromise—not your faith or your beliefs, but the things that aren't critical to eternity. Come up with a plan for how you will handle your differences. Never turn on each other. Lean, yes. Turn, no.

_____

_____

_____

_____

_____

_____

_____

_____

_____

_____

_____

_____

I believe in the Father, Son, and Holy Spirit.
I commit myself to serving You, Lord.
Help my fiancé and me as we get to know each other.
Give us the spirit of reconciliation when disagreements arise.
Be forever in our midst.

What values do you and your fiancé share in common?

_____

_____

_____

_____

_____

_____

_____

_____

_____

_____

_____

_____

_____

_____

_____

_____

PERSONALITIES

*Do everything without complaining or arguing,
so that you may become blameless and pure, children of God
without fault in a crooked and depraved generation,
in which you shine like stars in the universe.*

PHILIPPIANS 2:14–15

If you've ever done a study of the four basic personalities, then you already know that people come in a variety of personality packages. Perhaps you're a strong-willed leader type. What happens if you marry someone who needs a little prodding? What if you're outgoing, loud, and fun-loving and marry someone who tends to be more introspective and even occasionally wears his feelings on his sleeve?

Personality conflicts are inevitable, particularly if you're marrying someone with your same traits. Can you imagine two strong-willed leaders in the same house? Talk about head-butting! And what about two laid-back types? Would anything ever get done?

As you and your fiancé get to know each other—really get to know each other—take time to discover your personalities. Read up on the strengths and weaknesses of each one. Understand that you each have your own way of operating. And also understand that God has uniquely gifted each of you with your very own personality. You're not meant to be alike! And you will never function the same.

In other words, you will have to learn to work together. Your personality could very well determine a variety of things, such as how you work through problems or how you face the emotional challenges of parenting. What a great sense of humor God has. Get ready, bride-to-be!

Thank You, God, for the distinct personalities You have placed within me and my fiancé.
Help us to work together as one yet cherish each other's uniqueness.

What are some of the challenges of going from "me" to "we"?

_____

_____

_____

_____

_____

_____

_____

_____

_____

_____

_____

_____

_____

Methods of Expressing Love

This is how God showed his love among us: He sent his one and only Son into the world that we might live through him.

1 John 4:9

God expressed His love for us by sending His Son, Jesus, into the world. He's all about "showing" love. So how do you express your love for your fiancé? Are you a gift giver, showering him with little treasures to show him how you feel? Do you like to spend quality time with him? Do you lift him up with encouraging words? Whatever your method of expressing love, you need to be prepared for the fact that it's probably not the same way in which your husband-to-be will show his love for you. Don't assume he's not showing his love for you just because he expresses it differently. If he loves to cuddle, giving hugs and kisses whenever possible, he is showing his love for you through physical touch. You may be more inclined to love him by helping him with an everyday errand, such as picking up groceries or filling his tank with gas.

Regardless of the way you show your love for him, pay attention to the way he shows his love for you. Chances are, he is already showering you with love in his own special way.

One of the best things you can do before you get married is to find out what makes each of you feel most loved. This is part of having a sacrificial and giving relationship. When you learn to put your partner first and show him love in the way he most appreciates, he will know that he is loved. He will understand that he is important to you, and he will in turn do whatever it takes to show you that you are important to him, as well. Putting each other's interests ahead of your own is a godly way to build a loving and lasting relationship and ensure that both you and your future husband know that you are loved!

Lord, open my eyes to the ways that my fiancé shows his love for me.
Help me to receive this love and learn the best way to return it to him!

In what ways do you show your fiancé
that you love him?

_____

_____

_____

_____

_____

_____

_____

_____

_____

_____

_____

_____

_____

SECTION FIVE:

PRESERVING PURITY

Since, then, you have been raised with Christ, set your hearts on
things above, where Christ is seated at the right hand of God.
Set your minds on things above, not on earthly things.

COLOSSIANS 3:1–2

It's hard to imagine yourself as "pure" no matter how good you are. Sin itself separates us from God. But praise the Lord! The blood of Jesus, poured out on the cross at Calvary, cleanses us from all unrighteousness, bringing us back into relationship with God—despite any sins we have committed either before the engagement or after. This includes sexual sins.

Any man and woman in love with each other will find that issues of purity often rise to the forefront. Even before your engagement, you'll need a plan for how you will handle sexual temptations. It's not that sex is bad—it's not, you know.

Sex was created by God to be enjoyed by married couples and as a means to bring children into the world. In fact, the Lord came up with the idea of sex long before you were created and made it a desirable thing for people in love. You've been created with a sex drive.

That's why it's so important to be careful not to enter into sexual union before marriage. It is truly a gift for married partners. This truth is backed up by the Word of God, which openly discusses the pleasures of sex only between husband and wife. Like all gifts, however, sex can be mishandled or abused, which is why you need to be particularly careful.

So how do you resist the temptation to enter into this sacred union before you are married? As the verse above suggests, you can start by setting your mind on things above. It is possible to think beyond the sexual temptations—to put yourself in a different frame of mind.

It's worth the wait, bride-to-be. Your wedding night will truly be a night to remember! And if you've already crossed this line, don't be afraid to ask for forgiveness—then begin again. Covenant with the Lord to keep yourself pure from now until your wedding day. Such a decision will bring honor to Him and will give you something very special to look forward to!

But We're Getting Married!

*It is God's will that you should be sanctified:
that you should avoid sexual immorality; that each of you should
learn to control his own body in a way that is holy and honorable.*

1 Thessalonians 4:3–4

Even the staunchest supporter of sexual purity might struggle once the engagement period begins, seeing himself or herself as "already married in God's eyes." But that's not how the Lord sees it. To have sex before you're married cheapens the very idea of what God had in mind for you all along.

So make a resolution to remain sexually pure during the engagement period, and then commit your decision to the Lord. Next, communicate your decision to your fiancé. Once you're both of the same mind, decide how you're going to handle temptations when they come.

Entering into sexual union will link your spirits, as well as your bodies, and the Lord intends such a union only for marriage partners. So don't steal the beauty of the honeymoon. You can hang on a bit longer—and it will be worth the wait.

Did you know that people who choose not to have sex before marriage have healthier and happier marriages? There is also some thought that if you open the door to sexual immorality before marriage, that mindset (thinking sex outside of marriage is okay) will follow you into your marriage, making you or your spouse more vulnerable to an affair. So stand firm and resist temptation, understanding that God's will for you—His perfect will—is that you enter into this union only after marriage.

_Lord, give me the courage to decide to remain sexually pure,
regardless of any temptations. Help me not to view myself as "married" just yet._

Where do you and your fiancé stand on the issue of purity?

_____

_____

_____

_____

_____

_____

_____

_____

_____

_____

_____

_____

_____

BOUNDARIES

But among you there must not be even a hint of sexual immorality,
or of any kind of impurity, or of greed,
because these are improper for God's holy people.

EPHESIANS 5:3

Once you and your fiancé are committed to a purity covenant, you can take some very practical steps to avoid putting yourselves in a compromising position during this special God-ordained season. For example, when you're planning an evening out, make sure you set up a plan for the whole evening, with no major gaps. You might find yourself filling in the gaps with inappropriate actions if you're not careful. And guard your alone time. Place yourselves in group atmospheres as much as you are able. It also helps to find a friend or pastor to whom you can be accountable.

Talk with your fiancé about physical boundaries—what is and isn't appropriate. Have a serious "this far and no farther" conversation. Make sure you both agree; otherwise, the heat of the moment might just sweep you away.

The problem is, once boundary lines are crossed, it's hard to turn back. And if you slip up in this area, it's hard not to let it happen again.

The Word of God is full of "boundaries" stories. The Lord wants to protect His people, so He puts safety measures in place to do just that. If you're struggling in this area, read about the armor of God in Ephesians 6. Talk about safeguarding! If you keep yourself fully clothed in His armor, you will protect yourself from the advances of the enemy, who would like nothing more than to taunt and tempt you in the area of sex before marriage.

Boundaries: They're a good thing— a gift, even. Use them to your advantage, bride-to-be.

_____

_____

_____

_____

_____

_____

_____

_____

_____

_____

_____

_____

_____

Show me Your take on boundaries, Lord.
What does that word mean to You as it relates to the purity covenant
between me and my fiancé?

How have you handled sexual temptation during your engagement period?

_____

_____

_____

_____

_____

_____

_____

_____

_____

_____

_____

_____

_____

Overcoming the Past

"Come now, let us reason together," says the LORD.
"Though your sins are like scarlet, they shall be as white as snow;
though they are red as crimson, they shall be like wool."

ISAIAH 1:18

When you get engaged, you begin a new chapter in the life of you and your fiancé. Your upcoming marriage is an opportunity to start a brand-new life together, regardless of where either of you has come from. It is the chance to make a bright future together.

But what if you have a past you're ashamed of? What if your husband-to-be has a sexual history that he isn't proud of? Can you possibly start your marriage with a clean slate? Of course you can! The fact is, nearly every person you will meet has a sinful past. Battling with drugs, smoking, partying, even making mistakes in past relationships—everyone is bound to be ashamed of something from days gone by.

So how can you start fresh in your upcoming marriage? Don't focus on the past. Once you have asked for forgiveness and changed your behavior, you are no longer labeled by your former sins or mistakes. The same goes for your fiancé. It is okay to discuss your past issues with each other so that you can maintain an open and honest relationship, but don't dwell on the things that have already been dealt with and forgiven, or you will be miserable. Regardless of what has already happened, God is perfectly capable of wiping your slate clean if only you will ask for His help. As you and your future husband prepare to be married, talk about any past issues that may be haunting you. Pray together and ask God to give you a new beginning as you embark on your new life together.

God, please give me a fresh start.
Wipe my slate clean as I prepare to begin my new life with my future husband.
I ask You to forgive me as I forgive others.

What are your thoughts on your commitment to each other?

_____

_____

_____

_____

_____

_____

_____

_____

_____

_____

_____

_____

_____

THE HOLY HONEYMOON

Do not arouse or awaken love until it so desires.

SONG OF SOLOMON 2:7

The Bible is clear—the Lord created sex. He's all for it—between married couples, of course. He longs for your union to be one of the most special, intimate times of your life. Your honeymoon is meant to be holy. But how do you transition from being abstinent to being sexually active over-night? According to the scripture above from the Song of Solomon, love isn't meant to be "awakened" until its time. Can you really switch gears that quickly? Hang on, bride-to-be! That time is coming. . .soon.

What happens when love is awakened? If you've managed to abstain from sexual relations until now, you're sure to be on a learning curve on your wedding night, but don't worry! There are plenty of great Christian books on the subject if you need counsel. Also, don't be afraid to ask your married girlfriends or sisters for their advice. You will also want to visit with your doctor if you have any questions about family planning or physical issues.

Above all, relax! Don't spend much time fretting over what your husband might think about your flabby thighs. Instead, understand that he will see you as beautiful, because you are his. And know that God, the Creator of all, stands prepared to guide you, as well. Does it seem strange that you could actually ask the Lord to help you through the process of becoming sexually active? It shouldn't! He longs for you to turn to Him with every concern, every question. And He has even given you a "textbook" of sorts—the Song of Solomon—to let you know He has placed His stamp of approval on the union of a husband and wife.

_____

_____

_____

_____

_____

_____

_____

_____

_____

_____

_____

_____

Lord, I find myself facing fears and doubts related to my wedding night.
Calm my anxiety, give me wisdom, and walk me through this process.

What is your idea of the perfect honeymoon?

Song of Solomon: God's Ultimate Plan

My lover spoke and said to me, "Arise, my darling, my beautiful one, and come with me."

SONG OF SOLOMON 2:10

God has ordained your love life as sacred and intends it to remain so for the duration of your married life. As you come together in this special union, you are creating a bond that has spiritual significance. Entering the wedding chamber is compared in the Word of God to entering into the throne room of God, being ushered into His presence.

Of course, coming together in the marriage bed is part of God's plan for procreation (carrying on the human race), but did you ever think about the fact that He could have come up with another plan, something altogether different? Something less. . .well. . .fun?

The Lord wants you to enjoy your husband (after your marriage, of course) in every conceivable way, and that includes intimately. Yes, you will likely have children together, and your physical union will eventually result in the growth of your family. But whether you have children or not, you are still called by God to maintain a healthy sex life. That means you need to remain diligent in this area, even when you've been married for years.

It's probably hard to imagine now that you might one day grow weary of being intimate with your mate—that you might see it as a duty instead of a joy—but it's possible. Once the children start coming and you're exhausted from working all day, you might not feel like "giving of yourself" to your husband. And that can work both ways. But if you commit this area to prayer and strive to remain intimate with each other (both emotionally and physically), your marriage will thrive.

Father, You know my worries, fears,
and questions concerning my love life after marriage.
Give peace to my heart and grow me into the loving wife You have created me to be.

As a couple, where do you see yourselves
ten years from now?

_____

_____

_____

_____

_____

_____

_____

_____

_____

_____

_____

_____

_____

_____

SECTION SIX:

ADDRESSING THE TOUGH STUFF

Love is patient, love is kind. It does not envy, it does not boast,
it is not proud. It is not rude, it is not self-seeking,
it is not easily angered, it keeps no record of wrongs.

1 CORINTHIANS 13:4–5

Wherever two or more are gathered. . .there shall be conflict?

Yep, that seems to be the case, particularly when you're addressing the tough stuff. Some issues are just harder for couples to get through than others. Take finances, for instance. Disagreements often arise whenever financial issues rear their head. And heaven help you if you face a financial lack! Even the strongest of Christians can melt down quickly when faced with serious money-related woes.

What about family planning? Maybe you're an only child and are hoping for a houseful of children. Perhaps he's from a large home and would prefer a small family. Have you discussed this matter in detail? Don't wait until you're married!

Here are a few other tough issues you might as well face head-on: in-laws. What role will your in-laws play in your life? How involved do you want them to be? And what about your parents? Are you planning to stay close to them, gleaning from their wisdom, asking their opinions on every little thing? Do you and your fiancé differ when it comes to the role in-laws should play in your new life together? You'd better settle those differences now!

And what about wedding-related conflicts? Who will get their way when it comes to disagreements over how the wedding planning should move forward?

There are certainly many different things you could argue over during your engagement, if you were prone to argument. That's why it's important to get these things out in the open now, and to talk about them in a calm, assertive manner. Don't run from the tough stuff, bride-to-be! Face these issues head-on. You will get through it with the Lord's help. He knows what it's like to deal with the tough stuff, after all. He has to deal with our hearts every day, and that has to be tough work!

Checks and Balances

Do two walk together unless they have agreed to do so?

Amos 3:3

Money might not be the root of all evil—but the love of money certainly is! Perhaps that's why so many relationship troubles arise over finances. Dealing with money issues can be tough, but never more so than when you marry.

Maybe you come from a family where finances were always handled with great care. Pennies were saved for a rainy day. Your parents cut back on luxuries such as eating out, going to the movies, and so on. What will you do if your fiancé has a completely different mind-set? Maybe he grew up in a home where parents threw caution to the wind. Perhaps they lived off credit cards and never worried about paying the piper until he came knocking on the door.

Are you and your future husband in agreement on how bills will be paid and credit card debt handled? Will he be writing the checks, or would you like to take charge of this duty? Have you opened joint checking and savings accounts? Have you made a vow to discuss buying big-ticket items before they are actually purchased? If you've decided to have children, have you given any thought to the possibility of being a stay-at-home mom? What effect will that have on your finances?

If you are having trouble coming to agreement on any of these issues, consult a financial planner sometime after the wedding. Remember, money problems can add a great deal of stress to a marriage, so it's a good idea to take as many preventative measures as you can before trouble starts.

So address the tough stuff now, and ask God to help you through the process. And don't forget about tithing. Giving the firstfruits of your income to the Lord is a surefire way to set out on the course of financial security.

_____

_____

_____

_____

_____

_____

_____

_____

_____

_____

_____

_____

_____

Lord, today I commit to give our finances—and our attitudes surrounding them—to You. Give us wisdom and discretion in our spending.

How do you differ from your fiancé when it comes to handling your finances?

_____

_____

_____

_____

_____

_____

_____

_____

_____

_____

_____

_____

_____

Family Planning

By wisdom a house is built,
and through understanding it is established.

PROVERBS 24:3

After you and your fiancé are married, it will be only a matter of time before the big question comes up: "So when are you two going to start having babies?" Your parents will undoubtedly begin asking for grandchildren; your siblings will want nieces and nephews. But what do you and your husband want? This is the ultimate question, and it can be discussed before you get married.

When planning your future family, you'll find that many factors will come into play for both you and your husband-to-be. How many children do you want? How many does he want? Do you want to have children right away, or will you wait? Will you space your children out, or do you prefer to have them close together? Can you afford to have a child? Or two? Or three? These are questions you will want to answer before you get married.

As you discuss your thoughts on family planning, don't forget to include the ultimate family planner—God. After all, He is the one who gives life. He already knows how many children you and your future husband will have. He knows their names, the color of their hair, and their personalities. He knows exactly what you both need when it comes to children, and He knows when you need it. So take some time to pray with your fiancé, and give all of your desires and dreams for a family to God. He will take care of the rest!

_____

_____

_____

_____

_____

_____

_____

_____

_____

_____

_____

_____

_____

_____

Praise God! You are the ultimate family planner. You know everything about our future children. Be with us as my fiancé and I discuss our family plans. Help us come to a joint decision as we talk about our future together!

Have you and your fiancé discussed having
children—and how small or large you'd like
your family to be? To what degree are the
two of you in agreement on this matter?

_____

_____

_____

_____

_____

_____

_____

_____

_____

_____

_____

_____

_____

In-Laws and Out-Laws

Above all, love each other deeply, because love covers over a multitude of sins.

1 Peter 4:8

Who's in and who's out when it comes to in-laws? Do you love your parents but barely tolerate his? Wish his parents were your own? Are you happy to have parents at last, if you didn't grow up knowing your own mother or father?

A host of feelings may sweep over you as you realize you're not just marrying the man—you're marrying into a family. And that family, wonderful as it might be, is bound to be different from your own. Perhaps they're strong-willed, hoping to impose their ideas on you. "If it worked for our family, it's good enough for you." Maybe they're open and accepting, ushering you in with genuine smiles and well wishes.

What are you going to do if your mother-in-law is the sort to show up unannounced, hoping to help decorate your apartment? What if she insists on bringing some of your husband's favorite dishes by, along with copies of the recipes? Will you flinch or accept her help with joy? On the other hand, what will you do if she acts disinterested in the wedding and the marriage altogether? Different people have different ways of viewing things, after all.

First of all, remember that you all love the same man—your husband/their son (not necessarily in that order, depending on whom you ask). Putting this truth into perspective helps, doesn't it? You all want the best for him, and ultimately that means you all want the best for both of you. If you do run into complications, set up a plan of action with your husband-to-be. Discuss boundaries, if necessary. Let your in-laws know that there's always an open door; however, you won't be passing off a key. Above all, pray that the Lord will give you a genuine love for one another, and remember—any differences, even the big ones, are resolvable when love leads the way.

Thank You, Lord, for the gift of my future in-laws!
Give us all patience, wisdom, and understanding
as we develop a new relationship with one another.

What role will in-laws play in your life together?

_____

_____

_____

_____

_____

_____

_____

_____

_____

_____

_____

_____

_____

HABITS AND HOBBIES

A fool shows his annoyance at once,
but a prudent man overlooks an insult.

PROVERBS 12:16

If someone were to ask, "Do you have any bad habits?" how would you respond? Likely you'd excuse (or scarcely notice) your own habits—good, bad, or otherwise. Will your fiancé do the same? Has he already asked you about some of your quirky habits? What about his? Does he have any habits that might be tough to overlook? The things you find cute about your mate when you're dating are often the same things that drive you crazy once you're married. But what sorts of things are we talking about? These days, people habitually do all sorts of things that others might find strange: sleep with the television on, leave dirty dishes in the sink for days on end—the list goes on.

Yes, habits are going to become an issue at some point along the way. So are hobbies. Is your husband-to-be a sports fanatic? Addicted to video games? Do you like to spend money on scrapbooking supplies or CDs? Hobbies, while fun and relaxing, can separate a couple quickly. They can also get rather expensive and might interfere with your joint budget.

As always, you'll have to compromise. But how do you go about that? You don't want to lose your individuality, right? And if your hobby is something usable to the body of Christ (for example, playing an instrument on the worship team or working on the church's computer network), then it's important to strengthen that gift. If hobbies or other interests are coming between you, find something you both enjoy. Work toward a common goal. Enjoy time together doing fun and creative projects. In short, have a blast—together!

Thank You, Lord, for giving me someone who appreciates (and will help me with)
my habits, even the quirky ones. I praise You for giving me someone
whose interests will help me grow as an individual and a child of God.

What have you and your fiancé learned about each other during your engagement?

_____

_____

_____

_____

_____

_____

_____

_____

_____

_____

_____

_____

_____

_____

Conflict Resolution

Many waters cannot quench love; rivers cannot wash it away.

SONG OF SOLOMON 8:7

As you continue planning your big day, you and your husband-to-be will undoubtedly face a few disagreements. When the battle lines are drawn, will you fight fairly or lose your temper and insist on getting your own way? Is your fiancé the kind to give in easily, or will he stay up for hours on end, arguing until you finally give up?

When conflicts arise, don't worry. They are part of life and must be faced. Handling these conflicts in the right way is what will help to build a stronger relationship for your future.

When you face a conflict with your fiancé, talk through it calmly. Explain your side of things, but be willing to listen to his opinions, as well. Let him know that you care about his feelings on the matter by hearing his side of the story. Try to come to a workable compromise for whatever decision you are facing. Remember that you won't always be right. (Just because something looks or feels right to you doesn't necessarily mean it's right for both of you.) Be willing to admit when you are wrong, and ask for forgiveness. You will be surprised at how quickly a humble attitude can stop an argument.

Bride-to-be, you will soon discover your Prince Charming isn't always as charming as you'd hoped. He's human. Truthfully, even in the best of marriages, spouses will have times of disagreement. The question is, what will you do when problems arise? The answer is simple, really: Instead of focusing on Prince Charming, focus on the Prince of Peace. He alone has the answers to any problems you and your fiancé might face—either now or as a married couple. Ask Him to show you your fiancé's point of view and to help you put his feelings before yours. God will walk you through your conflicts if only you will take them to Him.

_____

_____

_____

_____

_____

_____

_____

_____

_____

_____

_____

_____

When I face a disagreement with my fiancé, give me the humility to bring it to You,
Lord. And help us to resolve it in a godly way.
Thank You for always being there for me, through good times and bad!

How will you handle disagreements once you're married?

_____

_____

_____

_____

_____

_____

_____

_____

_____

_____

_____

_____

_____

_____

PREWEDDING JITTERS

"Who of you by worrying can add a single hour to his life?"

MATTHEW 6:27

When you think about your wedding day, do you get nervous? If so, what are you nervous about? Concerned you won't fit into the dress? Nervous about standing up in front of a crowd? Afraid the ring bearer won't cooperate? Worried the family members won't all get along? Anxious about the wedding night?

There are countless things you could choose to worry about, but the Bible teaches that doing so is detrimental both to your spiritual life and to your health! The reason so many brides fret over their wedding day is that they've put tremendous effort into making everything perfect, yet so many things are simply out of their control.

How you handle your nerves is very important on the big day. You don't want to be like the "bridezillas" you hear about on television. Taking your nervous energy out on your bridesmaids, parents, or husband-to-be isn't the answer. So what do you do instead? How do you handle those last-minute jitters? Start by taking a deep breath! Realize that your memories of your wedding day will be great, even if everything doesn't go exactly as planned.

And if you're still nervous when you walk down that aisle, simply focus on your husband-to-be, keeping your eyes firmly locked on his. And keep your heart in tune with the Lord's. He has promised never to leave you or forsake you. He will give you the peace you need to have not only a glorious day, but a glorious life!

Here and now I give my worries and fears over to You, Lord.
Please calm my nerves and surround me with the peace
that surpasses all understanding!

Do you have any prewedding jitters? Why or why not?

_____

_____

_____

_____

_____

_____

_____

_____

_____

_____

_____

_____

_____

_____

IT'S TIME TO CELEBRATE!

"He will rejoice over you with singing."

ZEPHANIAH 3:17

Have you ever contemplated the word *celebrate*?

According to merriamwebster.com, the word means "to honor (as a holiday) especially by solemn ceremonies or by refraining from ordinary business, or to mark (as an anniversary) by festivities or other deviation from routine." In other words, a celebration is a special day when you set aside all normal activities in order to "mark" something significant.

Your wedding day is coming, bride-to-be! You're going to mark one of the most important days of your life! You have earned the right to celebrate, and God adds His joy to yours as the day draws nearer. Your engagement period is a season of celebration, too. Think about that! The Lord intends for you to spend these weeks and months as a "set apart" time, one you will remember for the rest of your life.

So what will you do to make this time in your life special? You might start by keeping a journal or scrap-booking several photos of you and your fiancé, as well as your bridal party and relatives. You can also celebrate your remaining time with your family. Make every moment count. And, of course, you can enjoy showers and parties thrown by loved ones. Celebrating the big day will be great fun, and you'll have plenty of opportunities to celebrate God's goodness throughout your engagement.

However you choose to mark this season, remember that the Lord is singing over you, having quite a celebration of His own. You've made His heart very happy, and His joy spills over, filling every heart!

Celebrating Family

I have been reminded of your sincere faith,
which first lived in your grandmother Lois and in your mother
Eunice and, I am persuaded, now lives in you also.

2 Timothy 1:5

You are who you are at least in part because of your family members. They have helped shape you into the beautiful woman of God you have become. And you'll want to keep them close, even after marriage. Celebrate your family, bride-to-be! The Bible is filled with examples of families celebrating together. Whole families. Fathers, mothers, aunts, uncles, grandparents, and siblings. It's fun to surround yourself with those you love (and who love you), and involving them in the planning of your wedding is a great way to do that.

So how can you include family members in your wedding experience? Start by celebrating your parents, especially if they're both still actively involved in your life. You will bring honor to them by recognizing their wisdom. They still have a lot to teach you, even now. You'll also want to make sure you express your gratitude often, particularly if they're paying for the wedding. To show them your gratitude, write a letter of appreciation—not just to acknowledge the things they're doing to help with the wedding, but to thank them for being great parents.

As for extended family members, you'll find that it's fun and easy to include people! Likely you have an aunt or grandmother who has all of the family addresses. Maybe she'd like to help you with the invitations. Perhaps she also has a book of family recipes she'd like to share with you.

The Lord loves family togetherness—before and after marriage. Plan some special family dinners. Create an environment where everyone can come together. Celebrate those you love!

I praise You for the family You've given me,
and now I ask for Your input on how to celebrate them during this special season!

In what ways have your families been supportive as you've planned your wedding?

_____

_____

_____

_____

_____

_____

_____

_____

_____

_____

_____

_____

_____

_____

CELEBRATING IN STYLE

Surely goodness and mercy shall follow me
all the days of my life.

PSALM 23:6 KJV

Women have always loved a good party—and weddings seem to provide the perfect opportunity! What fun it is to gather together with the women you love for an afternoon or evening of celebration. And what fun they will have ushering you into your new life—giving you the tools you'll need (toasters, pots and pans, home décor, lingerie, etc.) to move forward. It might seem a bit odd to you, having so much poured on you so fast, but it's part of the process—and a fun part, at that!

Did you ever think about the word *shower*? What does it mean to shower the bride with gifts? It means to lavish them upon her in such a way that she needs an umbrella to catch them all! And the word *blessing* leads the way. Your friends and family members want to bless you during this special time in your life.

So...let them! You're in a receiving season, bride-to-be. Don't be surprised if people pour out their love in a variety of ways. As you come together for these parties and bridal showers, don't be afraid to get silly. Play games. Let the party happen!

God loves to watch His children celebrate. He celebrated over you on the day you were born, and He's enjoying the party as you make this latest transition. In fact, He's celebrating over you right now!

_____

_____

_____

_____

_____

_____

_____

_____

_____

_____

_____

_____

_____

Thank You, Lord, for blessing me so abundantly with good friends and family members.
As I receive all of this attention and these gifts, give me a receptive heart
and show me what I can do to bless the givers in return.

What was most memorable about your bridal shower?

_____

_____

_____

_____

_____

_____

_____

_____

_____

_____

_____

_____

_____

_____

Celebrating Your "Sisters"

Greater love hath no man than this,
that a man lay down his life for his friends.

JOHN 15:13 KJV

As you begin today's devotion, take a moment to think about the special women God has placed in your life. Think of your very best friend and the role she has played. Look back over your years in high school and college and remember the friends you made. God always placed exactly the right people in your life at the time when you needed them most—and vice versa. Consider your mother and grandmother, your aunts, and other female relatives. Haven't they been an awesome addition to your life? And what about your coworkers? Surely even in the workplace you've developed special friendships. Finally, contemplate the women at your church—young and old. Can you see what a blessing they've been?

Your engagement provides the perfect opportunity to focus on the women in your life—your girlfriends! Some will be in your wedding party (or play a role in the wedding or reception in some fashion). Most will likely be in your life for years to come. But your engagement season provides the perfect time to let them know how much they mean to you.

Celebrate your "sisters," bride-to-be! Take them on individual outings for a bit of last-minute "single girl" time together. Send them cards. Have a blast watching them try on bridesmaid dresses. Make sure they know how much you love and appreciate them. Finally, make plans to continue your relationship once you marry. Don't ditch them once you're happily wed (especially the single ones). As much as you love your husband-to-be, you were never meant to build your life around one person. God created "His girls" to be sisters. Celebrate them!

_____

_____

_____

_____

_____

_____

_____

_____

_____

_____

_____

_____

_____

_____

_____

_____

What a wonderful plan You had—to give me "sisters" in the Lord—
women I can relate to on so many levels. Thank You for these precious sisters.
May You bless them abundantly!

How have your friendships changed now that you're engaged to be married?

Celebrating God's Goodness

The goodness of God endureth continually.

PSALM 52:1 KJV

Do you feel it, bride-to-be? Can you sense it? It's the goodness of God pouring over you!

There are so many ways to stay mindful of God's goodness, lest you forget about it. For example, when people are happy for you at the news of your engagement—even people you don't know—soak it in! It's part of God's goodness. When people wish you well, let their words serve as a precious reminder of the Lord's happiness.

Another way to stay aware of the goodness of God during this season is to look for and notice the beauty of the wedding-related items you're picking out. Take your flowers, for instance. Can't you just see God smiling at their beauty? Or your dress. Exquisite! Don't just think about the cost, but examine—*really* examine—the beauty.

The greatest gift you and your fiancé will receive as a wedding gift is God's goodness. It's part of the package. And as you prepare for your big day, bear in mind that you're celebrating an ancient ritual ordained by God. He has always been keen on weddings. In fact, Jesus' first miracle took place at a wedding.

Of course, the best way to remember God's goodness is by keeping Him first in your life. Remember, He was at the center of your life before you met your fiancé, and He needs to stay at the center now. He has been so good to you! Delight in the blessings you're receiving, and realize that God is the one who instigated all of this goodness. Enjoy, and don't forget to praise Him!

_____

_____

_____

_____

_____

_____

_____

_____

_____

_____

_____

_____

_____

Lord, as I meditate on Your goodness, my mouth is filled with praise!
Thank You for blessing me so abundantly. I rest in Your peace and Your presence.

How has God blessed you during your engagement?

_____

_____

_____

_____

_____

_____

_____

_____

_____

_____

_____

_____

_____

_____

CELEBRATING WITH YOUR GUESTS

"So the servants went out into the streets and gathered all the people they could find, both good and bad, and the wedding hall was filled with guests."

MATTHEW 22:10

Surely you're looking forward to not just your wedding, but also the reception that will follow. You've likely spent a good deal of time and money preparing for it. Wedding receptions are wonderful, because they give you an opportunity to relax after the ceremony and to greet your guests.

What do you think of when you hear the word *reception*? The word *receive* comes to mind, doesn't it? Your wedding reception is the perfect time for your family to receive your groom into the family, and for his family to receive you. The family circle is getting bigger, and that calls for a party! Your wedding reception is the perfect place to celebrate—not just your marriage, but your guests! After all, it's your first social event as a married couple, your very first party together. You are host and hostess—together (the first of many functions yet to come).

So what can you do to make the event special for your guests? Start by mingling. Sure, you'll be busy cutting cake and making toasts, but don't forget to say hello to the folks who drove miles and miles to be there. Openly appreciate your guests; let them know how much they mean to you. Enjoy their company. Have a good time and relax! Take the opportunity to thank your parents, in-laws, and other people who worked extra hard to put the wedding together.

Your guests will have a blast at your reception. After all, it's in human nature to celebrate—and that comes from our celebratory Creator!

Father, thank You for giving us so many people—friends, family,
and coworkers—who will be celebrating with us at our reception.
I thank You, Lord, for each and every one of them.
May Your favor and blessings rest upon them.

What do you think will be most memorable about your wedding reception?

_____

_____

_____

_____

_____

_____

_____

_____

_____

_____

_____

_____

_____

CELEBRATING THE GIFT OF EACH OTHER

Every good gift and every perfect gift is from above.

JAMES 1:17 KJV

Your wedding will be a time to celebrate your love for your fiancé, but the real fun begins for both of you when the ceremony is complete and you can begin your lives together. Remember, after the wedding day ends, the honeymoon begins! What a wonderful time to celebrate the gift of each other. It is a time to get to know each other as you have never been able to before. When you think ahead to your honeymoon, your first thought will likely be the physical intimacy you and your new husband will experience together. And although this is probably the most exciting and beautiful beginning to your new relationship, it is not the only thing you have to look forward to.

Regardless of where your honeymoon takes place, be it a tropical island or a hotel in your hometown, you can make it special by focusing solely on each other.

Take time to relax and enjoy each other, both physically and emotionally. Try not to overload your schedule with activities, and don't worry about the plans you have made. Be sure to schedule plenty of alone time, whether that means spending a day dressed in your pajamas, cuddling together in your room, or eating dinner on your balcony without anyone else around. When you do make plans, be willing to do things your new spouse might enjoy. Most of all, have fun together, regardless of what you are doing.

God has specifically given you this special honeymoon stage in your marriage to help you get off to a great start. He desires for you and your new husband to delight in each other, physically and emotionally. Take this time to savor the gift He has given you in your new spouse!

_____

_____

_____

_____

_____

_____

_____

_____

_____

_____

_____

Ah, the honeymoon. Like the icing on the cake!
Thank You, Lord, for my new spouse and for making our honeymoon
a special time for just the two of us. Show us ways to enjoy each other
during this exciting new time in our life together!

What traditions can you begin together as a family on your honeymoon?

_____

_____

_____

_____

_____

_____

_____

_____

_____

_____

_____

_____

_____

_____

SECTION EIGHT:
YOUR WEDDING DAY

As a bridegroom rejoices over his bride,
so will your God rejoice over you.

ISAIAH 62:5

*Y*our big day has arrived at last! You've planned for a beautiful ceremony. All of the players are in place: pastor, bride, groom, bridesmaids, groomsmen, flower girl, ring bearer, candle lighters, soloists, and so on. What happens next is out of your hands.

The flowers have been selected and gathered into bouquets, boutonnieres, corsages, and centerpieces. Your father (or brother, mother, or other special relative) is prepared to give you away. You've written your vows (or left that part up to the pastor). You've purchased your wedding rings, and your beautiful wedding dress is about to make its debut.

In short, you've done all you can do. In fact, you've worked long and hard to get it all done!

Now the culmination of all your work is about to be realized. And everything suddenly appears to be moving at warp speed. You thought this day would never get here, and now it feels as though the clock has cheated you!

So what do you do? How can you get through this day—one of the most important days of your life? For starters, breathe! In, out, in, out. Lay aside details as much as you're able, and count on those around you. God has strategically placed them in position to get the necessary jobs done. Yes, things are mostly out of your hands now, but isn't it just like God to plan it that way? After all, He works best when we reach the point where there's nothing left we can do, right?

Enjoy your special day, bride-to-be! May it be everything you've hoped for, dreamed of, and ever desired. May you look into your new husband's eyes and see a bright, happy future—one the two of you will share for many, many years. Above all, may you see this day as a "covenant" day—a day the Lord has created with the two of you in mind.

GIVING AWAY THE BRIDE

Therefore shall a man leave his father and his mother,
and shall cleave unto his wife: and they shall be one flesh.

GENESIS 2:24 KJV

On your big day, your father (or someone else you love) likely will "give you away" to your groom. You're probably looking forward to walking down the aisle on this person's arm, but did you ever think about the origin of this tradition?

The age-old custom of giving away the bride started when women were considered property. In fact, the groom often had to pay a price to "purchase" her. Can you imagine?

Aren't you glad things have changed? Thank goodness your family doesn't own you—at least not in the traditional sense! But how wonderful that the custom of giving away the bride has endured as a beautiful symbol of your family's passing the torch to your groom.

For much of your life, you lived under the authority of your parents. You resided in their home, ate their food, spent their money, lived by their rules. Now a power shift is taking place. As your father (or other loved one) places your hand in your mate's, a transition of sorts is taking place. It is an outward sign to all of your guests that your family loves, respects, and trusts this man, that he is (in their eyes and the eyes of all watching) worthy of you.

Giving away the bride is a part of "leaving and cleaving." It's symbolic. You're leaving one family and starting one of your own. And as you are "given away," imagine that the Lord has placed His stamp of approval on this transition, as well. What a beautiful thought!

_____

_____

_____

_____

_____

_____

_____

_____

_____

_____

_____

_____

_____

_____

_____

I praise You, Lord, for the transition I am making.
Help it to be a smooth one by easing my doubts and calming my fears.

Who will be giving you away on your wedding day?
What does this custom mean to you?

_____

_____

_____

_____

_____

_____

_____

_____

_____

_____

_____

_____

_____

The Veil

*Jacob served seven years for Rachel; and they seemed unto him
but a few days, for the love he had to her. And Jacob said unto Laban,
Give me my wife, for my days are fulfilled, that I may go in unto her.*

GENESIS 29:20–21 KJV

Modern brides have plenty of options when it comes to wedding veils. Long. Short. Beaded. Plain. You can find them in all sorts of styles and designs.

Whether you wear a veil with your wedding dress or not, it's fun to think about where the idea of the veil came from. Most people believe the custom of veiling a bride dates back to the story of Jacob, Leah, and Rachel, found in Genesis 29. In this unique story, Jacob is promised one bride (Rachel, whom he loves) but inadvertently ends up with another (Leah, through a switcheroo performed by her father). Talk about a fiasco!

These days, the idea of a groom "unveiling" his bride to make sure he has the right girl sounds a little funny, doesn't it? Can you imagine someone cheating your husband out of his intended (you)? Certainly not! Twenty-first-century brides often wear a veil as a symbol of their innocence and virginity. There's also something rather significant about the word *veil*. When the veil is lifted, it's as if you are saying, "I have nothing to hide. I'm going to be transparent with you." Symbolically, anything hidden between the two of you is made visible once the veil is lifted. And that's how it is in our relationship with God, too. The veil in the temple was torn in two when Jesus died on the cross, and we now have access into the throne room of God. What a beautiful picture of the bride of Christ, unveiled for her groom!

Thank You, Lord, that there is nothing to hide. All things are made visible.
Keep my relationship with my husband transparent—all the days of my life.

Do you plan to have a traditional wedding ceremony?
Why or why not?

_____

_____

_____

_____

_____

_____

_____

_____

_____

_____

_____

_____

_____

The Vows

For you have heard my vows, O God;
you have given me the heritage of those who fear your name.

PSALM 61:5

One of the most special and intimate moments of your wedding ceremony is when you and your husband-to-be take your vows. This part of the celebration is usually the most emotional. It is a time when you and your fiancé get to speak directly to each other, making a commitment to love and cherish each other for the rest of your lives.

You can make this part of your ceremony special in many ways. Most brides and grooms recite standard vows, which are usually repeated after the pastor officiating the ceremony. Still others choose to write their own vows. These original vows can be anything you like. You can write a letter to your fiancé, telling him what he means to you. Some brides and grooms even choose to sing a song to their future spouse as a vow of love. These are each beautiful ways of expressing your love and commitment to each other.

However you choose to state your commitment, whether through vows, a letter, or song, your ceremony will be special because you are taking the time to honor each other with your words and a lifetime commitment. As you speak your vows to your husband-to-be, be reminded that God has given him to you as a precious gift to be cherished, honored, and loved. You are giving yourself to him for the rest of your life, and that is the most beautiful and intimate commitment you can imagine!

As I take my wedding vows with my husband-to-be,
I thank You, God, for giving me such a priceless gift of love.
I make the choice today to love and honor my new spouse for the rest of my life.

Will you repeat the traditional wedding vows, or will you be writing your own? Why?

_____

_____

_____

_____

_____

_____

_____

_____

_____

_____

_____

_____

The Wedding Band

And now these three remain: faith, hope and love.
But the greatest of these is love.

1 Corinthians 13:13

Ah, the wedding ring! The moment it slides onto your finger, you've made your statement to everyone in attendance: "I'm his—for life! Nothing can separate us now." Your wedding ring is an outer symbol of an inner commitment—something for the whole world to see. It is your announcement that you are a married woman.

Did you ever wonder why a ring is the preferable piece of jewelry for a bride and groom? Why not a necklace or a bracelet? Traditionally, the wedding ring is made of a precious metal: gold, silver, or platinum. These are "pure" metals—metals tried by fire. They are precious and quite valuable. When your husband slips that band on your finger, he is saying, "You are of great value to me. You are precious to me!"

If you've given your heart to Christ,

your ring can represent something else, too. Like that ring, you have been purified, washed clean by the blood of Jesus. Your ring is a symbol of that purity. You enter your marriage as a chaste bride.

But why a piece of jewelry worn on the finger? Think of it this way: Your hands are always before you. In other words, they're in view most of the time, an ever-present reminder of the vows you've made. Your token of commitment is not a symbol you wear around your neck, where you might forget to look. Rather, it's clearly visible so that you never forget the covenant you've entered into with your mate. And it is a symbol of that circle of trust that now exists between the two of you.

_____

_____

_____

_____

_____

_____

_____

_____

_____

_____

_____

_____

_____

I praise You, Lord, for purifying me!
Thank You for the lifelong covenant I am entering into.
Make my ring a visible reminder of that precious commitment.

What does your wedding band mean to you?

Sealed with a Kiss

Let him kiss me with the kisses of his mouth—for your love
is more delightful than wine.

Have you ever heard the expression "sealed with a kiss"? When you kiss your groom at the end of your wedding ceremony, you are sealing the deal. But why a kiss?

The Word of God includes many references to kissing. A kiss is a beautiful outward sign of the love between two people, an appropriate symbol of physical union. And how interesting that the coming together of your lips also symbolizes the coming together of your thoughts and your actions. Your kiss signifies to those in attendance that you are together. You are "one."

And what a great way to end your wedding ceremony!

If you've ever been to the theater to see a play, you know what it's like at the end, when the audience rises to its feet and cheers. It's the "Ta-da!" moment. The roar of approval from the crowd is the satisfied response to what they've seen. This is the high point, the culmination!

When the pastor speaks those words you've waited to hear—"You may now kiss your bride!"—the same thing happens. The audience (symbolically) rises to its feet, cheering you on. The "Aha!" moment has arrived. You have sealed the deal—your union—till death do you part.

In much the same way, God places His seal of approval on your union. See His joy, His happiness, as a kiss of sorts. The ultimate covenant maker, He stands in agreement with you and your husband. The deal is sealed. *Forever.*

"Ta-da!"

_____

_____

_____

_____

_____

_____

_____

_____

_____

_____

_____

_____

_____

_____

Father, as I contemplate the "culmination" of our ceremony,
I praise You for bringing my husband and me together as one.
I praise You for the "Ta-da!" moment.

What are you most looking forward to during your wedding ceremony?

_____

_____

_____

_____

_____

_____

_____

_____

_____

_____

_____

_____

_____

_____

CUTTING THE CAKE

I am the bread of life.

JOHN 6:48

A wedding wouldn't be a wedding without a wedding cake. Right? Whether or not it's multi-tiered, elaborately decorated, and topped with a bride and groom, the cake is an essential part of any contemporary wedding reception.

But have you ever pondered why? Ever given any thought to the wedding cake? Cakes are the center of attention at a variety of celebrations: birthdays, anniversaries, and so forth. Perhaps the reason is that cake is a form of bread. In essence, it is symbolic of the substance of life—with sweetness!

Over a thousand years ago, a funny tradition evolved. The bride would actually have a cake broken over her head! (Can you imagine?) After eating a few bites, the groom would do the honors. This custom symbolized both her current virginal state and his (now) dominance over her. Wow! How would you feel if this tradition still existed?

A variety of other traditions involving wedding cakes and pies can be found in cultures around the world, but today the simple act of cutting the cake and feeding it to each other remains the most popular. When you give each other that first bite, you are saying to those in attendance, "We will feed each other"—in every sense of the word.

If cake is truly little more than "sweetened bread," then it should remind us of something else, too. According to the Word of God, Jesus is the Bread of Life. If you, as a couple, partake of that sweet bread, you will never go hungry!

In that sense, you really can have your cake and eat it, too!

_____

_____

_____

_____

_____

_____

_____

_____

_____

_____

_____

_____

As I read Your Word, feeding on the Bread of Life,
I marvel at Your goodness and revel in Your presence.

How did you choose your wedding cake?

_____

_____

_____

_____

_____

_____

_____

_____

_____

_____

_____

_____

_____

Tossing the Bouquet

My lover is to me a cluster of henna blossoms
from the vineyards of En Gedi.

SONG OF SOLOMON 1:14

Ever wondered why brides carry bouquets? Legend has it that medieval brides didn't get to bathe very often and opted to carry flowers on their wedding day to improve their body odor. In England, the bride and her attendants were ushered into the church by a little girl, whose job it was to drop flower petals (thus the tradition of today's flower girls), an action symbolizing a happy, "flowering" life. Many other cultures have a history of flowers at weddings, as well, each with its own meaning.

Flowers signify romance. They also represent love and caring. And there's something about the scent of flowers that just seems to make women smile.

When your wedding ceremony is over and the reception is drawing to a close, it's time for one of the most exciting events of the day—the bouquet toss! This tradition is not just about lavishing attention on the next woman supposedly to get married; it's about sharing the joy of your new marriage with all of your family and friends.

Just as you toss your bouquet as an invitation for your guests to have the same happiness you have, God offers an invitation for a "fragrant" relationship with Him to those who may not yet know Him. He desires for every person to experience the joy of salvation. As you share the joy of your new marriage with your closest friends, be reminded of the love God has for each of His children. He longs for a relationship with each and every one!

_____

_____

_____

_____

_____

_____

_____

_____

_____

_____

_____

_____

_____

Today as I shared the joy of my new marriage with those I love,
I was reminded of how much You love Your children.
Thank You for Your precious love, Father, and for Your pursuit of me.

What kind of flowers did you choose for your wedding? Why?

_____

_____

_____

_____

_____

_____

_____

_____

_____

_____

_____

_____

_____

CREATING YOUR
HAPPILY-EVER-AFTER

*Know also that wisdom is sweet to your soul; if you find it,
there is a future hope for you, and your hope will not be cut off.*

PROVERBS 24:14

Do you believe in happily-ever-afters? If you grew up reading fairy tales, no doubt you do. Perhaps you envision yourself living in a castle with your Prince Charming, where all of the bills are paid and servants care for your every need. Whether you're blissfully idealistic or not, you probably think life with your husband will be heavenly every moment of every day.

Truthfully, marriage is hard work. Your prince will—gasp!—actually look and act a bit more like a frog at times. And you're not always going to come across as his flawless princess. Over the years, you will discover each other's quirks and find plenty of reasons to disagree, even bicker.

However, this doesn't mean you can't have your own happily-ever-after. On the contrary! You just have to remember that the real Prince Charming is Jesus Christ—King of kings and Lord of lords. And if you keep Him in His proper place—at the center of your marriage—your relationship will thrive despite any complications.

One of the things you will have to establish right away is your role as a team member. You're on the same side, even when it doesn't feel that way. You are no longer two separate people, staring in two different directions. You are one flesh, gazing off into the distance together. Keep your prayer life strong—as a couple and as individuals. And when tough times do arise (and they will), guard your heart. Keep your temper in check. Never go to bed angry.

Above all, especially when times are tough, remember why you fell in love in the first place. And never forget that your union brings great pleasure to the heart of your Father. He longs for you to have a wonderful life together!

FAITHFULNESS—A LIFESTYLE

Let love and faithfulness never leave you; bind them around your neck,
write them on the tablet of your heart.

PROVERBS 3:3

What does it mean to be faithful to your mate? When you speak the words "keeping myself only unto him," are you referring just to something sexual, or is more involved?

Being faithful to your spouse is first and foremost a mental thing. It's a decision you make, one you must never stray from. Jesus knew (and taught) that unfaithfulness begins in the mind. For His views on the subject, check out the Gospel of Matthew, chapter 5. The mind is the battlefield, the place where trouble begins. So you have to make a decision that you will not allow your mind to "go there." Looking elsewhere (even for affirmation, compliments, etc.) is not an option. God has called you to be faithful in thoughts, actions, and attitudes—even when it's hard and even when your spouse isn't affirming you in the way you think he should.

There are many ways you can betray your spouse, many areas the enemy will target. "Not betraying" your husband doesn't *just* mean you won't have sex with someone else. It means you won't betray private information, private thoughts, or (basically) anything your friends and family members shouldn't know. Above all, it means that you will keep your heart turned in the direction of your spouse and not elsewhere.

The Word of God is clear in this area: God requires faithfulness. It is an act of direct obedience to Him. Make up your mind as a new bride to live in faithfulness to your spouse—and to God—all the days of your life.

Lord, in my union with my husband, may I be found faithful.

Protect this area of my marriage as I commit it to You for safekeeping.

What does faithfulness to your spouse mean to you?

_____

_____

_____

_____

_____

_____

_____

_____

_____

_____

_____

_____

_____

ATTITUDE–THROUGH THICK AND THIN

Your attitude should be the same as that of Christ Jesus.

PHILIPPIANS 2:5

Probably the most important commitment you will make during the exchange of your wedding vows will be these words: "for better or for worse, in good times and in bad." This commitment is sure to be tested at some point in your marriage, most likely sooner rather than later.

How do you make it through rocky times, when disagreements arise, when you feel like arguing, or when compromise seems unattainable? The answer—it's all about your attitude! Remember, your attitude is a choice, and according to the scripture above, you are called to choose to have the attitude of Christ. By taking on His attitude instead of your own, you will alter the outcome of most misunderstandings.

Sometimes when you feel like arguing with your husband about something trivial, you just need to make the decision to let it go. Keep an open mind, and be willing to admit when you're wrong. Remember, you don't always have to be right. In fact, admitting your mistakes and asking for forgiveness will undoubtedly help your spouse open up to you and admit the areas in which he is wrong. This openness can ultimately lead to the end of a disagreement and a great time of making up!

There will be difficult times in your marriage. That's life. But God desires for you to handle these moments with a good attitude. When you face tough situations with a godly attitude, you will open up the door for healing and restitution and, ultimately, a healthy marriage.

_____

_____

_____

_____

_____

_____

_____

_____

_____

_____

_____

_____

_____

Lord, I know You desire for me to have an attitude of humility in my marriage.
Help me face tough situations with a godly attitude,
and bring restitution to any disagreements that may arise.

How do you and your spouse handle compromise?

_____

_____

_____

_____

_____

_____

_____

_____

_____

_____

_____

_____

_____

Don't Let the Sun Go Down on Your Anger

"In your anger do not sin":
Do not let the sun go down while you are still angry.

EPHESIANS 4:26

When arguments arise—and they will—it's important to know how to handle them with humility and an attitude of forgiveness. God gives you a fresh start each day in your marriage, so no matter what you faced the day before, you always have the opportunity to begin anew. But if you go to bed angry with your spouse, it's impossible to start the next day with a clean slate.

"Don't let the sun go down on your anger" isn't just an old adage; it's biblical truth! If you and your spouse have a disagreement, the best thing you can do is talk about it and get it resolved before your head hits the pillow. It's critical to make your feelings known and reconcile with your spouse. When you let grievances fester inside of you, you are opening the door for the enemy to take hold of your thoughts toward him. The longer you let your anger build, the more resentment you will have toward each other. When you resent your spouse, you are literally lying next to someone with whom you are not united spiritually or emotionally, and that is never a good thing.

Talk through your feelings about the situation. Do whatever it takes to resolve the disagreement before you go to sleep. When you allow an opportunity for healing and forgiveness before you go to bed, you will have the peace of knowing that you are lying next to someone who truly cares about you and whom you truly love. And the next morning will bring a bright beginning to a brand-new day!

_____

_____

_____

_____

_____

_____

_____

_____

_____

_____

_____

_____

Lord, may I never go to bed angry.
Remind us to come to You in prayer before talking to each other about our feelings.
Then allow us a time of healing and forgiveness before sleep.

How do you and your spouse settle disagreements?

_____

_____

_____

_____

_____

_____

_____

_____

_____

_____

_____

_____

A SENSE OF HUMOR

A merry heart doeth good like a medicine:
but a broken spirit drieth the bones.

PROVERBS 17:22 KJV

What does a sense of humor have to do with a good marriage? Everything! A smile. A playful wink. These are the things that can turn even the most strained situation around in a heartbeat. And having a merry heart is good for you, as the scripture above indicates. In fact, it's a great stress reliever!

Imagine you've been invited to a holiday celebration at your in-laws' house. You've offered to bring a particular food item. But you're not very good in the kitchen—at least not yet. The dish doesn't turn out well, but you decide to take it anyway. When you arrive, both you and your dish are the subject of many a joke. The teasing doesn't seem to stop. In fact, your failed attempt is brought up at every holiday get-together from that time onward.

How would you handle this situation? As a new bride, you might not be smiling. And your heart might not be merry. Perhaps you're the type whose feelings get hurt easily, particularly when it comes to family-related matters. But both you and your spouse will find that learning to laugh at yourselves (as individuals and as a couple) will help you jump many hurdles!

The partnership you have with your spouse will give you plenty of opportunities to develop your sense of humor. Will you stand up to the test? Will you commit to keeping a merry heart, even when the bills are overdue, the children are crying, and people are criticizing you?

Remember, the Bible also says that the joy of the Lord is your strength. Keep that song in your heart! It will take you far.

What a blessing to know that You desire us to be merry.
Help me, Lord, not to take things too seriously
and to remember that Your joy is my strength.

What does your spouse do to make you laugh?

_____

_____

_____

_____

_____

_____

_____

_____

_____

_____

_____

_____

_____

INTIMACY

How delightful is your love, my sister, my bride!
How much more pleasing is your love than wine,
and the fragrance of your perfume than any spice!

SONG OF SOLOMON 4:10

What does it mean to be intimate with your mate? Is it just a matter of coming together in sexual union, or is there more to it? Perhaps it would help to think of the word *intimate* as meaning "into your mate." When you're into something, you want to learn all about it, every possible detail. You want to make it your own, to enjoy it.

And lest you think intimacy is purely about the physical and sexual, think again. Being intimate with your husband means that you truly care about the things he cares about. And think about this: The word *intimate* isn't tossed about lightly—unlike the word *love*. You hear people say it all the time: "I love peanut butter!" "I love pizza!" "I love the beach." "I love my kids." But you never hear someone say, "I'm intimate with peanut butter."

The word *intimate* is special. Private. Significant. Reserved. Set apart for something that the world doesn't spend a lot of time thinking about or dwelling on. But our God is an intimate God. He knows us. He's into us. And He longs for us to be into Him, as well—not just as individuals, but as a couple.

Oh, how wonderful to be intimate with your spouse and your God! Can you think of a more complete individual than that? To allow yourself to know and be known by both a mate and your Maker—now that's really something!

_____

_____

_____

_____

_____

_____

_____

_____

_____

_____

Lord, I love my spouse and treasure our times of intimacy together.
You have made such intimacy possible.
Now, as I take time to enter into intimacy with You, I feel surrounded by Your love.
Lord, I want to know You—to really, truly know You.

What does intimacy mean to you?

_____

_____

_____

_____

_____

_____

_____

_____

_____

_____

_____

_____

_____

What God Has Joined Together

"Therefore what God has joined together, let man not separate."

MARK 10:9

When you and your husband-to-be stand before a crowd of people and speak your wedding vows, you are entering into a covenant with each other. A public covenant, no less. Repeating the words "till death do us part" is easy on your wedding day. But just wait until you've lived together ten, twenty, or thirty years! As much as you hate to see it happen, the "fluffy" part of romance tends to get pushed to the side. Children are born. Houses are purchased. Bills must be paid. Job issues need to be addressed. And somewhere in the middle of it, you might find yourself forgetting about the two of you.

Your marriage is meant to last forever. It's a covenant agreement, one you don't enter into lightly. God takes this agreement between a man and a woman very seriously, as evidenced by the scripture above. It is His desire that you remain a couple until the very end of your lives.

So once you take your vows, how do you plan to stay committed to your spouse? The most important thing you can do is realize that love is a choice. There will be days when you won't feel like loving your husband, but you keep working at it. You make a conscious decision to love him no matter what happens. You stay determined to work at your relationship, regardless of any issues that may arise.

God does the joining, and He longs for that covenant to "stick." So even in the tough times, hang in there! The Lord will keep your relationship strong as long as you place Him in the very center of it.

_____

_____

_____

_____

_____

_____

_____

_____

_____

_____

_____

_____

_____

_____

_____

_____

Dear God, You have brought my spouse and me together and made us one.
Give us Your heart concerning the covenant of marriage.
Give us the strength and will to maintain a healthy, strong,
and loving relationship and to view our union as a commitment
for as long as we both shall live.

How do you keep your relationship a priority?

_____

_____

_____

_____

_____

_____

_____

_____

_____

_____

_____

_____

_____

Wrapping Up: What's Love Got to Do with It?

For God so loved the world, that he gave his only begotten Son,
that whosoever believeth in him should not perish,
but have everlasting life.

JOHN 3:16 KJV

Ah, love! Human beings around the globe are on a quest to find it. They search high and low. Can it be found in another person? In material possessions? In the eyes of a newborn babe? By looking within? Perhaps as a new bride, you feel you've finally come to understand the meaning of love. But have you?

What is *real* love, anyway? Where is it found? And what does it have to do with your marriage, your life together? Is it just a feeling, something that will fade over time, or does real love consist of something more?

One of the most beloved scriptures in the Bible—surely one of the most quoted—is John 3:16: "For God so loved the world that he *gave*" (emphasis added). That's what love does. It gives, and gives, and then gives some more.

Understanding what love has to do with it is simple, really. Love is the basis, the root, of your marriage. It is the glue that holds everything together. It's not just a feeling you have one day—a feeling that disappears the next. It's an eternal, never-ending gift, one you will never fully understand. Why is that? Because God *is* love. And He pours Himself on you as a couple. Lavishes you with Himself. Gives both of you His joy, His vision, His sense of purpose. And He does it all, why? Because He adores you. Both of you!

In fact, He adores all of His creation—so much that He sent His Son, Jesus, to die on the cross so that men and women everywhere could have eternal life. The "love" you're experiencing with your mate feels eternal, doesn't it? But it's just a sampling, just a foretaste of the "eternal" love we can have once we enter into covenant with God by accepting His Son.

If you (or your mate) have never asked Jesus to come into your heart and to be the Lord of your life, please take the opportunity to do so now, before you step out into your marriage. He longs for you to understand His love for you, and He wants to sweep you into His arms—for all of eternity.

Coming to know Him is simply a matter of acknowledging Jesus Christ and His work on the cross, then asking Him to take the reins of your life. Accept His free gift of salvation, and dive into the ocean of love He will pour out around you.

_____

_____

_____

_____

_____

_____

_____

_____

O Lord, I thank You for the love You showed me by sending Your Son, Jesus,

to die on the cross for my sins. I recognize that I am a sinner,

in need of Your saving grace. I ask You to be Lord of my life. I accept You as my Savior,

my "first love." Come in and sweep my heart clean.

Clear out any of the ugliness from the past. Make everything new again.

Wash me whiter than snow! Take the reins of my heart, Lord.

Grow me into the person You would have me become.

Grow me into the wife You would have me become.

Give me Your eyes to see situations the way You see them.

May I come to know the fullness of Your love, and may my marriage blossom and grow.

Teach me how to share that love with those who surround me

(my husband, family, and friends) and those yet to come

(my children and their children). I commit my life to You and ask that love—

real love—would lead the way in all I do. In Jesus' name, amen!

What is your definition of real love?

Recommended Reading
>*The Five Love Languages* by Gary Chapman
>*The Act of Marriage* by Tim and Beverly LaHaye

Wedding-Related Web Sites

General
>www.beachbrideguide.com
>www.allweddingcompanies.com
>www.blissweddings.com
>www.foreverwed.com/music/christianweddings.html
>www.my-wedding-blog.com
>www.onewed.com
>www.partypop.com
>www.theknot.com
>www.topweddingsites.com
>www.weddinggazette.com/links/0011.shtml
>www.weddings.myevent.com
>www.weddingsolutions.com
>www.weddingusa.com
>www.wednet.com
>www.yourwedding101.com

Cakes
>www.bhg.com/home/Wedding-Cakes.html
>www.bridaltips.com/wedding-cakes.htm
>www.topweddingsites.com/wedding_cakes.html
>www.wilton.com/wedding/index.cfm

Gowns
>www.alfredangelostores.com
>www.bargainweddinggowns.com
>www.bridalmartsuperstore.com/wedding_gown.html
>www.bridecouture.com
>www.davidsbridal.com

Honeymoon
>www.theknot.com/honeymoons

Reception/Décor
>www.reception-ideas.com
>www.superweddings.com/decor/decoranddesign1.html
>www.yourweddingcompany.com

Showers
>www.weddingshowergifts.com/resources/index.php